Untold Narratives

John.
   Thank you for your support on
This project
         Shaun.

Untold Narratives

African Americans Who Received Special Education Services and Succeeded Beyond Expectations

edited by

Shawn Anthony Robinson

Director of Pure and Complete Phonics

Independent Scholar

INFORMATION AGE PUBLISHING, INC.
Charlotte, NC • www.infoagepub.com

Library of Congress Cataloging-in-Publication Data

A CIP record for this book is available from the Library of Congress
http://www.loc.gov

ISBN: 978-1-64113-184-1 (Paperback)
       978-1-64113-185-8 (Hardcover)
       978-1-64113-186-5 (ebook)

CONTENTS

PART I

SETTING THE STAGE

PART II

TRANSFORMATIVE FRAMEWORK:
STORIES FROM AFRICAN-AMERICAN MEN

PART III

TRANSFORMATIVE FRAMEWORK:
STORIES FROM AFRICAN-AMERICAN WOMEN

PART IV

CULTURAL CAPITAL CLASSROOM ACTIVITY

FOREWORD

THE NARRATIVE EXPERIENCES OF AFRICAN AMERICANS WITH DISABILITIES

A Call for Critical Reflection

There is nothing wrong with Black students who are fortunate to learn
in an environment in which they feel valued and appreciated and are expected
to do great things academically.
—Kunjufu, 2012, p. vii

Marginalized, ostracized, and low academic achievement are words that have been used to describe what happens when African Americans go to school (Fashola, 2005; Polite & Davis, 1999). Furthermore, there is a widespread lack of knowledge when it comes to understanding the experiences of African Americans with disabilities in schools and society. A structural reformation of schooling practices has been proposed to bring about equity and equality in education, particularly for African Americans (Du Bois, 1994). Over the past several decades, we have seen a rise in important literary works that attempt to describe inequitable experiences in education and challenge the notion that African-American children are inferior. This book is a much needed contribution to that body of literature. The personal

Untold Narratives, pages vii–ix
Copyright © 2018 by Information Age Publishing
All rights of reproduction in any form reserved.

narratives presented in this book reflect the challenges directly related to current research concerning the norms, culture, and practices of education as we know it. Moreover, the narratives in this book as told through the voices of African Americans with disabilities reveal the concreteness of experiences juxtapose socially constructed ideals.

One might ask, how can a collection of personal narratives help inform my understanding? Personal narratives can offer many representations of self, create coherence among others, and offer insight into sociocultural patterns in a given set of social processes. Personal narratives can be insightful, about more than just one family or one person's story. Similarly, life stories can be an insight into cultural practices and norms. Culture, as the common thread and societal make-up of our existence, has been examined, explored, and correlated with ideals of behaviors, attitudes, and norms impacting the schooling experiences of those on the margins of power.

Social trends and changing demographics impact school culture and the politics of education. Select groups of students (particularly African Americans with disabilities) are at a disadvantage when schools enforce and maintain practices that do not consider the tangible stories and lived experiences of all students. As such *Untold Narratives* is for everyone. Teachers and school personnel, government officials, board of directors, and anyone else identified as key stakeholders in education must be made aware of the severe ramifications of how marginalization and discrimination plague the human race.

Access to education in U.S. schools mirrors the beliefs embedded within a democratic system of government. In our democracy, it is propitious that education laws are implemented to create a better world by fully endorsing the charters of freedom, including the Declaration of Independence, which explicitly states, "All men are created equal, that they are endowed by their Creator with certain unalienable Rights, that among these are Life, Liberty and the pursuit of Happiness." The Individuals with Disabilities Act, for example, was created to ensure equity and inclusive practices in the education and assistance of individuals with disabilities. Therefore, it is our duty to sustain and uphold these charters and work to eradicate racial prejudices altogether. These stories provide tangible examples of successful outcomes that have disrupted the status quo.

Many African Americans succeed despite persisting injustices. Nevertheless, a negative image is often painted that blames African-American students for their low achievement. This book advances the idea that African Americans with disabilities can and do succeed when afforded the opportunity to

1. rely upon culturally mediated best practices;
2. engage in critical dialogue around transformative frameworks as presented in such chapters as "Accessing Special Education: the Lived Experience of a Black Male with Learning Disabilities" and

"Insecurities of Special Education: What It's Like to Be Black, Male, and Learning Disabled"; and
3. reflect on the promises of reflective assessment of figured worlds as in such chapters as "It Can Be Done" and "Otosclerosis: The Invisible Disease."

This book moves us in the direction of a call to action that is synonymous with achieving equity in education. The personal narratives presented allow a reader the opportunity to assign meaning to the socially constructed categories of difference marked by ability as it intersects with race, class, and gender (Connor, 2006; Gillborn, 2015). African Americans with disabilities are confronted with a myriad of challenges stemming from racist and hegemonic policies and practices predating this era. However, in the present day we must encourage that stories like these be told in order to illustrate the struggles many Americans still face. We must understand the potential threat to all people if these stories remain untold.

—**Aaliyah Baker**

REFERENCES

Connor, D. J. (2006). Michael's story: "I get into so much trouble just by walking": Narrative knowing and life at the intersections of learning disability, race, and class. *Equity & Excellence in Education, 39*, 154–165.

DuBois, W. E. B. (1994). *The souls of black folk.* Mineola, NY: Dover.

Fashola, O. (2005). Developing the talents of African American male students during nonschool hours. In O. Fashola (Ed.), *Educating African American males: Voices from the field* (pp. 19–50). Thousand Oaks, CA: Corwin Press.

Gillborn, D. (2015). Intersectionality, critical race theory, and the primacy of racism: Race, class, gender, and disability in education. *Qualitative Inquiry, 21*(3), 277–287.

Kunjufu, J. (2012). *There is nothing wrong with black students.* Chicago, IL: African American Images.

Polite, V., & Davis, J. E. (1999). *African American males in school and society: Practices and policies for effective education.* New York, NY: Teachers College Press.

INTRODUCTION

UNTOLD NARRATIVES

African Americans Who Received Special Education Services and Succeeded Beyond Expectations

Shawn Anthony Robinson
Guest Editor

ACKNOWLEDGMENTS

This edited book would not have been possible without having a strong faith in God, staying encouraged, and understanding the true purpose of how this edited book may not only give students and parents hope, but also help change students' self-perceptions and belief in reaching their full academic abilities.

I am grateful to all the authors with whom I have had the pleasure to work with, and I appreciate their patience. I am especially indebted to the following colleagues for supporting this project and providing editorial assistance: Aaliyah Baker, PhD, assistant professor in the College of Education and Leadership, and Nina Weisling, PhD, assistant professor, language and literacy at Cardinal Stritch University; John Pruitt, PhD, associate professor of English at the University of Wisconsin-Rock County; and Richard C. McGregory, Jr.,

Untold Narratives, pages xi–xx
Copyright © 2018 by Information Age Publishing
All rights of reproduction in any form reserved.

PhD, Director of the Center for Study of Black Students at the Office of National Black Student Union and Executive Director of Strategic Communications and Academic Achievement of Robbinsdale Area Schools.

Nobody has been more important to me in the pursuit of this project than the members of my family. I would like to thank my wife, Inshirah, whose love and guidance are with me in whatever I pursue; my two sons, Jeremiah and Ezekiel, who will one day understand the importance of this book; and my mom, Michelle Myers. My family provided unending inspiration and are the ultimate role models. I also want to thank all my friends and colleagues who continuously uplifted me during this project.

DEDICATION

This edited book is dedicated to all those African-American (AA) or Black students defined by specific labels—learning disability (LD), blindness/visual impairment, cognitive development, speech or language impairment, and hearing impairment—both in and out of special education, who have been devalued and neglected, and had their learning framed by a deficit perspective. To the students who feel hopeless, I too felt there was no way out, but I stayed focused, encouraged, and dismissed those who told me what I could not do as an AA male in special education because of my learning disability. I want you to always believe in yourself and write your own story of triumph like these authors and I have. More importantly, find your purpose in life and pave it forward. I would also like to dedicate this book to the late Dr. Robert T. Nash, and all my Special education teachers who saw potential in me.

VOICELESS NO MORE: LET THE WORLD KNOW

I start this edited book with a poem titled "Let the World Know" because, as the authors expressed in their personal narratives, at one point someone discounted and treated them differently, and/or prevented them from achieving academically at high levels (Robinson, 2016a). The poem reflects a story of my navigating the special education system, feeling inferior, and having experiencing some teachers discounting my ability to succeed (Robinson, 2016b; 2017b).

> The negative perception that portrays Black males with dyslexia is a deception;
> An overreaction by teachers that leads to criminalization and legal action, instead of teaching fractions;
> Housed in special education with many days of frustrations;

Feeling rejected from the many years of being educationally
  neglected;

Curriculum that isn't particular to meeting their learning styles,
  which is concerning;

This limits their chances to advance academically, and they maybe
  experimenting on another level chemically;

They are discounted from being college-bound, but have the potential to turn it around;

The ones in special education that get an opportunity to shine, can
  redefine the stereotypes that have kept them behind;

Imagine starting college reading nine years behind, not thinking if
  you can survive, doesn't give one a peace of mind;

The description is written for you, with low level phonetic
  transcriptions;

Remedial classes, damages one's own self-perception and makes one
  feel less than the masses;

The gatekeepers don't see you as a high achiever;

Yet, it's possible to receive special education services, graduate, and
  narrate your own story;

To refute the mainstream fraudulent notion that assumes that Black
  males with dyslexia have no room to bloom;

My method of choice is a qualitative approach that allowed me to be
  creative and innovative;

I share my story of HOPE, so brothers in the trenches know how to
  cope;

I use my voice as a weapon of choice to inspire Black males with
  dyslexia to aspire, and to re-energize those that have been
  marginalized;

Now society will hear my voice (and others) that will give thousands
  of Black students in special education reasons to rejoice.

Moreover, reflected throughout this anthology are personal narratives that are creative, innovative, and inspiring. These authors' stories might give current students in special education reasons to rejoice. Therefore, this collection reflects a much-needed area of work for hearing the voices of African-American (AA) or Black students defined by various labels such as learning disability (LD), blindness/visual impairment, cognitive development, speech or language impairment, and hearing impairment. These students have been ignored, discounted, and silenced, and their learning framed from a deficit rather than a strength-based perspective while in the preK–20 educational system.

Further, as Connor (2006) notes, how students have understood their positions within the general education and special education systems has been limited. For me, Connor's assertion is personal, as I did not truly understand my own position within the special education system until I critically reflected on my past and connected those experiences to relevant literature as a student in a PhD program (Adams, 1990; Banks & Hughes, 2013; Renzulli, 2012). First, after searching through numerous academic databases, I continuously found the literature written from a western philosophy that excluded the authentic voices of AA students with a LD who had successfully navigated the special education system (Robinson, 2013). Second, this resulted in my dissertation chair encouraging me to compose an autoethnographic account that described my journey navigating the academic system through three perspectives: giftedness, race, and dyslexia (Robinson, 2017c). Last, this opportunity allowed me to challenge the status quo by writing my own narrative to counter the predisposition that society has about AA students with various labels in special education and after (Robinson, 2016c).

Thus, as I began this book project, I thought it needed to have at least 12 chapters by writers within only the traditional educational settings. However, after reflecting it became apparent that the quantity did not matter. What mattered were the different voices. I could be different, reach out to people not included in academic circles, and take a risk with this project as I wanted to provide a platform for others to write their own narratives (Robinson, 2017a). Further, what mattered to me was the quality of voices sharing their stories in ways that could reach current students in the special education system and their parents who felt hopeless or excluded (Robinson, 2016d). In fact, one author of this edited book shared an appreciation by stating:

> I heard your heart when we first talked about the project and understood that this was to be a practical tool to offer support and hope for those who follow. If I would have had something like this when I was matriculating and negotiating the school system life might have been very different. Thank you again for your tenacity and vision.

As I reflected on this comment, I became highly aggravated by how AA students continue to face educational obstacles despite the historical 1954 *Brown v. Board of Education* decision that aimed to change policy and practice and ensure an equal education for AA students, especially those with disabilities. The 1954 ruling caused school districts to reverse their policies of racial segregation, which violated the equal protection clause of the 14th Amendment to the United States Constitution (Albrecht, Skiba, Losen, Chung, & Middelberg, 2011; Hardman & Dawson, 2008). In other words, the *Brown* decision found that AA students were not receiving an education equal to that of their White peers. To help alleviate this inequality, the United States government passed the Title I Elementary and Secondary Education Act (ESEA), which ensured that students had access to a fair and equal opportunity to receive a high-quality education allowing them to meet at least proficiency on state academic achievement standards and assessments (Kaufman & Kaufman, 2005).

Yet, in the 21st century, we are still advocating for academic equality for AA students.

Therefore, I hope this book may help teachers across a wide array of academic disciplines who are interested in meeting the academic and social needs of current AA students within the preK–20 educational system. While this book will emphasize successful narratives, it will also provide counter-narratives to demystify the myth that AA students defined by specific labels cannot succeed or obtain terminal degrees (Robinson, 2016c).

PART I: SETTING THE STAGE

This book begins with what we know about the advancement of school policies and their impact on educating individuals with disabilities in the United States. However, even with these governmental policies established to protect and provide equal opportunities for all students, the reality for AA students is structural segregation, disproportionate representation, and lower academic standards. Furthermore, exploring these educational policies through the lens of critical race theory offers educators a chance to assess how race, law, and power indeed affect the academic advancement of these students within society and the system.

To start with a specific emphasis on special education in Chapter 1, "Historical Policy Analysis of Education Policies for Differently Abled in America," Fields and Roberts-Lewis discuss educational policies within the United States school system that have created access, services, and provisions for one group within the preK–20 pipeline, while marginalizing and creating barriers for others, primarily minorities. Overall, their chapter provides a historical review of educational policies impacting the education of students with disabilities, and the implications of these policies toward accessing a free and appropriate public education.

Furthermore, in the second chapter, "Structural Segregation, Disproportionate Representation and Disabling Assumptions in Special Education: A Black Educator's Narrative," Stewart and Kennedy analyze how racism has been used as a tool to segregate racially minoritized students in special education. Their examination reviews how school practices and policies within the contexts of the United States educational system continue to marginalize and produce barriers for minorities, which is similar to the assertion that Fields and Roberts-Lewis make in Chapter 1. Thus, critical race theory provided Stewart and Kennedy with the opportunity to use reflections and observations of an educator in a midwestern public school district who named and rejected the inequities forced upon racially minoritized students in special education.

The authors' chapter looks overall at the structural segregation, disproportionate representation, and teachers' disabling assumptions projected in special education classrooms. Further, they assert that more research is necessary to yield effective implications that will reduce the number of racially minoritized students in special education, and equitably matriculate them into mainstream classrooms.

PART II: TRANSFORMATIVE FRAMEWORK: STORIES FROM AFRICAN-AMERICAN MEN

Creswell and PlanoClark (2011) claim that the intent of a transformative framework is to "lift up the voices of participants and develop a call for action using data sources that can challenge injustices and provide evidence that is acceptable to stakeholders" (2011, p. 151). Students may become transformed and find their voices after completely understanding why literacy is necessary. The International Literacy Association (2017) defines literacy as:

> The ability to identify, understand, interpret, create, compute, and communicate using visual, audible, and digital materials across disciplines and in any context. The ability to read, write, and communicate connects people to one another and empowers them to achieve things they never thought possible. Communication and connection are the basis of who we are and how we live together and interact with the world.

What follows are narratives of authors who write from a transformative framework, each seeking to empower students in special education to realize that they can achieve what they never thought conceivable. Moreover, from a literacy perspective, the authors in this edited book who are now living with disabilities express how their interactions with the world influenced their identities and how they became academically successful.

As mentioned previously, Connor's (2006) analysis is critical when examining schooling practices and policies for AA students with disabilities, which authors Fields and Roberts-Lewis plus Stewart and Kennedy discuss in Part I. Mainly, how African Americans understand their position in the special education system is strikingly vague from traditional scholarship. Therefore, the three chapters of Part II counter the absence of the authentic voices of AA males with disabilities.

Abbott's story in Chapter 3, "Accessing Special Education: The Lived Experience of a Black Male with Learning Disabilities," navigates the challenges of his education. By sharing his lived experience with both physical and learning disabilities, he provides a counternarrative to the traditional narrative of why AA males in special education are often deemed "uneducable" by informing and empowering both students with disabilities and those who teach them.

Similarly, in Chapter 4, "A Voice Within: How Private Speech Continues to Propel One Man to Academic Success," Ewell reflects on the low expectations teachers had about his abilities. Moreover, he explains how their unconstructive philosophical beliefs toward his capability propelled him forward. At a young age he heard that "blind students could not succeed in integrated classrooms," and his parents were told that "they shouldn't dream of seeing their son graduate from high school with a diploma." But like other authors, he succeeded far beyond the early prognosis of educators, pediatricians, and physicians, and refused to be influenced by his experiences or others low expectations.

Chapter 5 draws similarities to Abbott and Ewell's stories; Sidney, like so many AA males with specific learning disabilities throughout their preK–20 schooling, faced various academic and social barriers (Robinson, Ford, Ellis, & Hartlep, 2016). His story "Insecurities of Special Education: What it's Like to be Black, Male, and Learning Disabled" stands out because we seldom hear the stories of these students who at one point were victimized by a system and eventually, through a combination of personal strength and interpersonal relationships, overcame the odds stacked against them. Sidney revisits his experiences being served by a special education program in a small district where teachers had a deficit perspective regarding his capabilities. Despite his obstacles, Sidney persevered through developing relationships and absolute resolve. Therefore, throughout the chapter he provides recommendations for educators and other advocates interested in developing positive outcomes for AA males with LD in similar circumstances.

PART II: TRANSFORMATIVE FRAMEWORK: STORIES FROM AFRICAN-AMERICAN WOMEN

The next three chapters are personal narratives of AA women with specific disabilities. Peterson (1997) explains that, "Given the dearth of research on the experiences of [African-American or] Black disabled women, there has subsequently been little in the way of formal theorizing on how gender and disability intersect with race" (p. 121). Peterson's study has implications because stories of Black women with "disabilities" are virtually absent. Also, Vernon (1999) asserts that "the intersection of race, gender and class in the experience of Black women has long been a debated issue" (p. 386).

To bring these narratives to the forefront, Cerillo describes her journey in Chapter 6, "It Can Be Done," as a student not only receiving special education services for her blindness, but also turning a "disability" into an ability. Cerillo's journey is one of hope and inspiration as students within the preK–20 academic system could benefit from learning about the strategies and services she utilized to become academically independent and successful. Moreover, based on her journey, she advocates for academic justice and serves as a living example that teachers can't limit students' abilities based on their physical limitations. Instead, she encourages teachers to help students tap into their giftedness in areas such as general intellectual ability, specific academic ability, leadership, and psychomotor learning (National Society for the Gifted & Talented, 2017).

In Chapter 7, "Otosclerosis: The Invisible Disability," Boone describes her academic experience without the ability to hear. Boone did not receive special education services, but her journey of hope, pride, and self-advocacy is one that many students enrolled in the preK–12 special education system can benefit from reading. She explains how (a) the severity of her "disability" and (b) "stigmas" of having a hearing loss could be perceived as a mental challenge or helplessness. However, Boone's story does highlight the struggles of an African American women with a hearing loss. She was resilient and exhibited many traits of giftedness throughout her journey. Furthermore, her story could provide motivation for current African American girls in special education who share a similar diagnosis. Overall, her chapter debunks the most common myths that hearing loss is a disease that consumes one's life. Hearing loss doesn't become an identity; those with hearing loss have the power to take their disability and define it themselves (National Association for Gifted Children, 2017).

In Chapter 8, we end with "Not About the Disability, But the Ability to Succeed," as Elufiede provides personal educational experiences based on lessons she learned through mentoring and accessibility to resources. Moreover, Elufiede reiterates a common theme throughout the collection, which focuses not only on the reconstruction of special education services, but also on legal and political implications for teaching, learning, rehabilitation, and employment. She, like many other authors, stresses that classroom strategies should focus on meeting students' learning needs (see Part IV).

REFERENCES

Adams, M. J. (1990). *Beginning to read: Thinking and learning about print.* Cambridge, MA: MIT Press.

Albrecht, S. F., Skiba, R. J., Losen, D. J., Chung, C. G., & Middelberg, L. (2012). Federal policy on disproportionality in special education: Is it moving us forward? *Journal of Disability Policy Studies, 23*(1), 14–25.

Banks, J., & Hughes, M. S. (2013). Double consciousness: Postsecondary experiences of African American males with disabilities. *Journal of Negro Education, 82*(4), 368–381.

Connor, D. J. (2006). Michael's story: "I get into so much trouble just by walking": Narrative knowing and life at the intersections of learning disability, race, and class. *Equity & Excellence in Education, 39*, 154–165.

Creswell, J. W., & Plano-Clark, V. L. (2011). *Designing and conducting mixed methods research* (2nd ed.). Thousand Oaks, CA: SAGE.

Hardman, M. L., & Dawson, S. (2008). The impact of federal public policy on curriculum and instruction for students with disabilities in the general classroom. *Preventing School Failure, 52*(2), 5–11.

International Literacy Association. (2017). *Why literacy.* Retrieved from https://www.literacyworldwide.org/why-literacy

Kaufman, M. J., & Kaufman, S. R. (2005). *Education law, policy, and practice: Cases and materials.* New York, NY: Aspen.

National Association for Gifted Children. (2017). *Definitions of giftedness.* Retrieved July 11, 2017, from https://www.nagc.org/resources-publications/resources/what-giftedness

National Society for the Gifted & Talented. (2017). *Giftedness defined.* Retrieved July 11, 2017, from https://www.nsgt.org/giftedness-defined/

Peterson, J. S. (1997). Bright, tough, and resilient—and not in a gifted program. *Journal of Secondary Gifted Education, 8*(3), 121–136.

Renzulli, J. (2012). Reexamining the role of gifted education and talent development for the 21st century: A four-part theoretical approach. *Gifted Child Quarterly, 56*, 150–159.

Robinson, S. A. (2013). Educating black males with dyslexia. *Interdisciplinary Journal of Teaching and Learning, 3*(3), 159–174.

Robinson, S. A. (2015). *Navigating the academic systems through three perspectives: A twice exceptional, black male, with dyslexia. An autoethnographic account.* (Unpublished doctoral dissertation). Cardinal Stritch University, Milwaukee, WI.

Robinson, S. A. (2016a). Can't c me. *Review of Disability Studies, 12*(4), 1–4.

Robinson, S. A. (2016b). *How coaching Special Olympics changed the trajectory of my life. Wisconsin English Journal, 58*(2), 166–175.

Robinson, S. A. (2016c). My otherness: Navigating and surviving predominantly White institutions. In D. Y. Ford, M. T. Scott, R. B. Goings, T. T. Wingfield, & M. S. Henfield (Eds.), *R.A.C.E. mentoring through social media: Black and hispanic scholars share their journey in the academy* (pp. 45–52). Charlotte, NC: Information Age.

Robinson, S. A. (2016d). Introduction. *Wisconsin English Journal, 58*(2), 76–80. Retrieved from https://wejournal.wordpress.com/2017/10/28/vol-58-no-2-2016/

Robinson, S. A. (2017a). "Me against the world": Autoethnographic poetry. *Disability & Society, 32*(5), 748–752.

Robinson, S. A. (2017b). Phoenix rising: An auto-ethnographic account of a gifted black male with dyslexia. *Journal for the Education of the Gifted, 40*(2), 1–7.

Robinson, S. A, Ford, D. Y., Ellis, A. L., & Hartlep, N. D. (2016). Introduction. *Journal of African American Males in Education, 7*(1), 1–4.

Vernon, A. (1999). The dialectics of multiple identities and the disabled people's movement. *Disability & Society, 14*(3), 385–398.

Yosso, T. (2005). Whose culture has capital? A critical race theory discussion of community cultural wealth. *Race Ethnicity and Education, 81,* 69–91.

PART I

SETTING THE STAGE

CHAPTER 1

HISTORICAL POLICY ANALYSIS OF EDUCATIONAL POLICIES FOR THE DIFFERENTLY ABLED IN AMERICA

Jody A. Fields
University of Arkansas at Little Rock

Kristie Roberts-Lewis
Point University

ABSTRACT

Educational policies in this country have been wrought with a mixed bag of opportunities and challenges. Often, policies that create access for one group often have deleterious impacts that disenfranchise others. In a political climate that promises "no child left behind," important policy considerations and options are crucial to ensure the viability of our country's educational systems to prepare the next generation of academically astute citizens. States began to pass compulsory education laws in the mid-1800s, and by 1918 all

Untold Narratives, pages 3–16
Copyright © 2018 by Information Age Publishing

states had compulsory education laws. Most states excluded children with disabilities, a decision upheld by the courts until the passage of the 1958 Expansion of Teaching in the Education of Mentally Retarded Children Act. The Elementary and Secondary Education Act of 1965 provided funds for students with disabilities. Section 504 of the Rehabilitation Act of 1973 sought to protect persons with disabilities against discrimination. The Education for All Handicapped Children Act of 1975 (EAHCA) provided funding to states to support educating students with disabilities. The reauthorization of EAHCA in 1990 inaugurated a name change to the Individuals with Disabilities Education Act (IDEA) establishing the requirement of a transition plan as part of a student's IEP by age 14. The last reauthorization occurred in December 2004. This chapter provides a historical review of educational policies on the education of children with disabilities in the United States since their inception through the 21st century and the implications.

Education is the responsibility of the states as implied in the 10th Amendment to the U.S. Constitution (Yell, Rogers, & Lodge Rodgers, 1998). States began to pass compulsory education laws in the mid-1800s based on the belief that if public schools are to be successful in socializing children, all children had to attend school (Sperry & Gee, 1998). The attendance rates of children from underserved communities was sporadic at best as many left early or did not attend at all. Compulsory attendance laws gave school officials the power to prosecute parents if they failed to send their children to school (Brown v. Board of Education, 347 U.S. 483, 1954; Cremin, 1970; Sperry & Gee, 1998, pp. 139–145). In 1834, the Pennsylvania Free School Act created a system of state regulated school districts and later a Department of Education to oversee the newly created schools.

The state of Massachusetts in 1852 passed its first compulsory school law followed by the state of New York shortly thereafter (Watson, 2008). As states began to pass compulsory laws, the number of public schools began to grow exponentially (Comer, 2004). By 1865, unfortunately, the new changes lacked structure on the level of education offered and inconsistency across all states due to the lack of uniform compulsory attendance required. Hence, schools throughout the 1800s were primarily focused on the preparation of students for citizenship and for earning a livelihood, with an emphasis on agrarian and the early industrialized society's sense of civilization and culture (Iorio & Yeager, 2011). General core educational requirements included reading, writing, and later spelling, geography, history, the U.S. Constitution, nature study, physical education, art, and music (Bohan & Null, 2007).

In 1893, a ruling by the state of Massachusetts Supreme Judicial ushered in an era when children with disabilities could be expelled despite the gains made by compulsory education. While laws were being passed to ensure educational opportunities for all children, social and political leaders were concerned about the effects of public education's growing diversity of immigrants while protecting the shared national cultural, norms, and values. Horace Mann proposed a solution to these social problems by recommending the establishment of common schools to be funded by tax dollars.

This recommendation was driven by Mann's belief that "when children from different social, religious and economic backgrounds were educated together, they would learn to accept and respect each other" (Wright, 2005, p. 7). Hence, curriculum within common schools focused heavily on "common values" that included self-discipline and tolerance for others. The outcome of such efforts was to ensure proper socialization of children and enhanced interpersonal relationships with the goal of improving social conditions (Cremin, 1970, pp. 183–194). When special education programs were introduced, they were structured as delinquency prevention programs for children deemed to be "at risk" who came from lower socioeconomic communities and backgrounds. Hence, schools in urban districts developed manual training classes to support their general education curricula with a focus on social skills, values, and norms. By 1890, hundreds of thousands of children were learning carpentry, metal work, sewing, cooking, and drawing in manual classes:

> Manual training was a way of teaching children industriousness, and clearing up their character problems... the appeal of this training was the belief that it would attract children to school, especially poor children, so their morals could be reshaped... Manual training would teach children to be industrious and prevent the idleness that accounted for the increasing crime rate... it could teach self-discipline and willpower. (Cremin, 1970, pp. 220–222)

EARLY SPECIAL EDUCATION PROGRAMS

Early special education programs also focused on the "moral training" of African- American children (Cremin, 1970, pp. 192–226). Unlike many other states, New York had an ambitious public education system advocating a proper education for all children (regardless of race, socioeconomic status, or disability) that would provide special industrial training preparing children for a useful vocation. The *New York Times* in 1908 noted that "educating children with hereditary or acquired disabilities one of the most important and humanitarian activities of the Board of Education, giving these children the benefits of a free education to which they are entitled" (Iorio & Yeager, 2011).

By 1918, all states had enacted compulsory education laws, but many excluded children with disabilities from schools, a decision upheld by the courts. These laws became progressively stricter until the Supreme Court's

Pierce v. Society of Sisters decision in 1925. In this case, the court held as unconstitutional an Oregon compulsory attendance law that made it illegal to attend any academic institution besides public school (Pierce, 1925). Later, *Wisconsin v. Yoder* (1972) affirmed the traditional interest of parents to opt out of compulsory attendance for religious reasons. During a White House Conference in 1910, the issue of education for disabled children was broached, suggesting that children with disabilities and/or special needs required remedial studies and support, hence inaugurating a movement away from the historical preference for an institutional placement model to one of the school-based services in segregated classes.

In other words, children with disabilities could be excluded from the general population in public schools. As a result, the number of segregated classes increased significantly between 1910 and 1930. When allowed to attend, children with disabilities were often segregated together in generic special education classes (Iorio & Yeager, 2011). Thus, because of schools segregating and distinguishing children with disabilities from "normal" children, special education classes were often held in off-site places such as trailers and school basements. Furthermore, many states permitted school authorities to exclude children (particularly those with disabilities) if it was determined that they would not benefit from an education or if their presence would be disruptive to others (Iorio & Yeager, 2011).

In response to the treatment and segregation of children with disabilities in public schools and the deplorable conditions they endured, parents organized advocacy groups to support each other and work for change. In 1922, the Council for Exceptional Children was established to advocate for children with disabilities and improve the educational experience of those with gifts and talents, or disabilities. At its inception, one of the primary goals was to organize and establish professional standards and to be a strong advocate for parents, teachers, and administrators of special education (Council for Exceptional Children, n.d.).

In 1958, the Illinois Supreme Court held that compulsory education laws did not apply to children with mental impairments. Until 1969, it was a crime in North Carolina for a parent to try to enroll a handicapped child in public school after the child had been excluded (Weber, 1992). Between the late 1950s and late 1960s, "the courts upheld legislation that excluded students whom school officials judged would not benefit from public education or who might be disruptive to other students" (Yell, Rogers, & Lodge Rodgers, 1998, p. 220). In the wake of the perceived discriminatory practices to segregate children with disabilities, by the early 1970s most states had laws in place requiring schools to educate children with disabilities.

Much of the perceptual change of the 1970s is rooted in the Civil Rights Movement. The 1954 case, *Brown v. Board of Education*, had a substantial impact on educational law (Turnbull, 1993). *Brown* was applied broadly and allowed the 14th Amendment to be applied to other populations because it included provisions that guaranteed equal protection for people as a class such as by race, gender, or disability:

> All persons born or naturalized in the United States, and subject to the jurisdiction thereof, are citizens of the United States and the State wherein they reside. No State shall make or enforce any law which shall abridge the privileges or immunities of citizens of the United States; nor shall any State deprive any person of life, liberty, or property, without due process of law, nor deny to any person within its jurisdiction the equal protection of the laws. (U.S. Constitution, Amendment XIV, Section 1)

The amendment forbids states from denying any person within its jurisdiction the equal protection of the law. In other words, if states provide education to its citizens, they must provide education to all its citizens including children with disabilities. The definitive court case gave parent advocates an avenue to seek redress for their children, and the outcome provided momentum for the equal opportunity movement: all children with and without disabilities should have access to an education.

As children were moved from institutions to public schools, segregation became the norm. While segregated classes allowed for smaller class sizes and individualized instruction, access to the general curriculum was not always permitted. Many students who would otherwise excel in a regular classroom setting were not included in a nonlabeled classroom setting. Such segregation and the undesirable locations of classrooms for children with disabilities led to the development and social engagement of a diversity of advocacy groups crucial to the development of special education as we know it today (Iorio & Yeager, 2011).

THE EXPANSION OF TEACHING IN THE EDUCATION OF MENTALLY RETARDED CHILDREN ACT

The first federal act targeting the education of children with disabilities occurred in 1958 with the Expansion of Teaching in the Education of Mentally Retarded Children Act, which required all schools receiving federal funding to provide handicapped children with equal access to education and mandated that they be placed in the least restrictive educational environment possible. The Elementary and Secondary Education Act of 1965 provided funds for certain categories of students, including students with disabilities (Moody, 2012).

In 1971, the Pennsylvania Association for Retarded Children (PARC) sued the Commonwealth of Pennsylvania for a state law that allowed public schools to deny education to certain children, namely those who had not "attained a mental age of 5 years" (Li, 2013). This law had been consistently used by the state to deny education to students considered too burdensome to integrate into school and classroom environments. The case was brought and settled before the District Court of the Eastern District of Pennsylvania. Based on the strength of evidence, the sides came to a settlement in 1972, and U.S. District Court Judge Masterson gave a consent decree deeming the former laws unconstitutional and tasking the state with providing a free public education to all children between the ages of 6 and 21 years. Additionally, the state was asked to provide sufficient education and training for all "exceptional" children, to the level of those given to their peers. In line with these new requirements, the Commonwealth could no longer deny any child with disabilities access to free public programs of education and training (*Mills v. Board of Education*, 1972).

In 1972 after the *PARC v. Commonwealth of Pennsylvania* decision, a case was brought before the U.S. District Court of the District of Columbia by the family and friends of Peter Mills and seven other children against the District of Columbia. Peter, a 12-year-old student with behavioral issues, was excluded from school because the district believed that his behavioral issues would be too expensive, estimating millions of dollars to provide services to him, thus presenting an undue hardship.

District Court Judge Joseph Waddy stated that no child eligible for a publicly supported education could be denied such education without an equal alternative tailored to the child's needs. In addition, the district's practice of excluding children with disabilities from education was deemed unlawful (Moody, 2012). Hence, the judge ordered the district to take the following actions: to provide an accessible, free, and suitable education for all children of school age regardless of disability or impairment; to refrain from suspending a child for more than 2 days without a hearing; and to provide all parties in the suit with publicly supported educational programs tailored to their needs (Mills, 1972).

REHABILITATION ACT OF 1973

Section 504 of the Rehabilitation Act of 1973 was enacted to protect persons with disabilities against discrimination based on those disabilities by requiring that school districts provide a free and appropriate public education (FAPE) to qualified students in their jurisdictions who had a physical or mental impairment that substantially limited one or more major life activity, regardless of the nature or severity of the disability. Under Section 504, FAPE means providing regular or special education and related aids and services designed to meet the student's individual educational needs as adequately as those of nondisabled students are met (U.S. Department of Education, 2010).

EDUCATION FOR ALL HANDICAPPED CHILDREN ACT

In 1974, Senator Harrison Williams of New Jersey stated that we are responsible for providing education for all children to meet their unique needs. Williams sponsored the Education for All Handicapped Children Act of 1975 (EAHCA; Yell, Rogers, & Lodge Rogers, 1998), which provided state funding to support educating students with disabilities. It mandated five elements: (a) nondiscriminatory testing, evaluation, and placement procedures; (b) least restrictive environment; (c) procedural due process; (d) free education; and (e) appropriate education. A central component of EAHCA was the establishment of individualized education programs (IEP; *Honig v. Doe*, 1988; Yell, Rogers, & Lodge Rodgers, 1998). This began a shift in recognizing that all students are general education students first and should have access to the general curriculum. According to programs such as the Elementary and Secondary Education Act (ESEA), Title I, English Language Learners, and special education should enhance students' access to the general curriculum, not replace the general curriculum.

Ultimately, the Education Amendments of 1974 (Public Law 93-380) were enacted to require states receiving federal funds to provide full educational opportunities for both children with disabilities and gifted and talented children. This was the first national initiative to meet the needs of both populations. Additionally, PL 93-380 highlighted and outlined specific due process procedures to ensure the rights of students with special needs and addressed the issue of providing education to students with special needs in the least restrictive environment. Unfortunately, the law was not sufficiently enforceable.

Despite the passage of a myriad of laws, specifically the passage of the EAHCA, a 1980 report by the Education Advocates Coalition on Federal Compliance Activities to Implement the EAHCA suggested that "many students simply were not receiving the education promised to them by the Act." Specifically, the report noted that many children were in the exact same position. Concomitantly, it was determined that many handicapped children were still not receiving educational services. Of those receiving services, a large number had not received an individualized evaluation or an IEP. In addition, many students were found to be unnecessarily segregated, and those in regular classes were often without the extra services promised to them (Education Advocates Coalition 1980, pp. 4–5). Five years after the passage of the act, the lives of many handicapped children remained basically unchanged. The authors of the report deemed this situation:

a national disgrace—a disgrace to the nation's millions of handicapped children and their parents who rely on enforcement of PL 94-142 [Education for All Handicapped Children Act] to provide for their children the opportunity to become independent, self-sufficient adults. It is also a violation of the trust of the United States Congress...And it is an affront to the nation's taxpayers who will ultimately bear the expense of these children's dependence and lack of skills. (Education Advocates Coalition, 1980, pp. 5–6)

According to the United States Department of Education, by 1984 fewer than 7% of all disabled students in the United States were being educated outside of public schools, and two-thirds of disabled children in public schools received at least part of their education in normal classrooms (Winzer, 1993, p. 382). Unfortunately, this finding does not mean that all students were receiving IEPs or receiving the extra services that they needed. In fact, the individual situations of many disabled students may have changed for the worse as they moved from specialized private learning environments into public school systems not fully prepared to teach them.

INDIVIDUALS WITH DISABILITIES EDUCATION ACT

The 1990 reauthorization of EAHCA (renamed the Individuals with Disabilities Education Act [IDEA]) included the recognition of autism and traumatic brain injury as separate disabilities and established the requirement of a transition plan as part of a student's IEP by age 14. Reauthorization in 1997 focused on improving performance and educational achievement. There was a mandate for students with disabilities to be included in statewide and districtwide assessments. Congress also required states to offer mediation as an option for dispute resolution. In December 2004, the reauthorization of IDEA was signed, and there were multiple clarifications and new requirements written into the act including the establishment of coordinated early intervening services (CEIS); state performance plans and annual performance reports (SPP/APR), summary of performance (SOP); the offering of resolution sessions in dispute resolution; and a change in the secondary transition age from 14 to 16 or younger.

The five elements established in EAHCA in 1975 have remained the foundation of IDEA. However, despite the safeguards in place for services to children with disabilities, many families still struggle with navigating special education programs at the local education agency (LEA). Families have rights embedded in IDEA. In *Your Child's Rights: 6 Principles of IDEA*, Saleh (n.d.) outlined "six major principles ... focusing on students' rights and the responsibilities of public schools to children with disabilities":

1. Free appropriate public education (FAPE): Participating states and territories of the United States of America are required under Part B of IDEA to ensure FAPE is made available to eligible children aged 3 to 21 with disabilities. Children are students in the general education program first, and special education and related services should be designed to support them in the general curriculum and meet their unique needs to better prepare them for postsecondary education, competitive employment, and independent living.

2. Appropriate evaluation: Local education agencies (LEAs) must conduct appropriate evaluations of students suspected of having a disability in a timely manner. The procedures in evaluating students for eligibility of special education and related services should be "nondiscriminatory in testing, evaluation, and placement" (EAHCA, 1975). Appropriate evaluations must be conducted by knowledgeable and trained evaluators using sound evaluative tools.

3. Individualized education plan (IEP): Each student found eligible for special education and related services, upon parent consent to serve, must have an IEP developed and implemented. Using the existing evaluations to inform the student's unique needs, the IEP team (which consists of parents/guardian, special and general education teachers, and related service providers) develops the written document that addresses a student's present level of performance, annual goals and objectives, classroom accommodations and modifications, and educational environment. If the educational environment is not in the general curriculum setting, then an explanation needs to be provided.

4. Least restrictive environment (LRE): A student with a disability should be served in the general education setting as much as possible. The IEP team must explore if classroom accommodations, supplemental services, and modified instructional methods would allow a student to remain in a regular classroom setting with nondisabled peers. According to IDEA, there is a continuum of educational settings, and the IEP team must make responsible and reasonable efforts to determine if the least restrictive environment is inside or outside the regular classroom. As noted previously in Principle 3, if the LRE is determined to be outside the general curriculum setting, an explanation must be provided.

5. Parent participation: IDEA specifically denotes that parents of a child with a disability have the right to participate in any decisions regarding their child's placement in special education and related services and in an LRE. IDEA requires that both the student and parent be invited to IEP meetings and establishes them as partners in the decision-making. Additionally, parents can refuse evalua-

tions, additional testing, and placement to receive special education services.

6. Procedural safeguards: As one of the original five elements of EAHCA in 1975, procedural safeguards ensure parents and students can enforce their rights under the law, as they protect parental access to educational information such as placement documents including evaluations and transition planning. Further, certain procedures in place can resolve disagreements between parents and the LEA: "Parents have a right to review all educational records pertaining to their child, receive notice prior to meetings about their child's evaluation, placement, or identification, and to obtain an Independent Educational Evaluation (IEE) for consideration at such meetings. If disagreements arise, parents have the right to [file a complaint], request mediation or due process hearings with state-level education agencies, and beyond that may appeal the decision in state or federal court" (Saleh, n.d.).

Families should be the biggest advocate for their children and need to understand their rights under IDEA. The safeguards are in place to protect them, while giving both families and school systems mechanisms to resolve disputes. IDEA gives parents the right to:

- receive a complete explanation of all procedural safeguards;
- inspect and review their child's educational records;
- participate in meetings related to identification, evaluation, placement of their child and the provision of FAPE to their child;
- obtain an independent educational evaluation;
- receive prior written notice on all meetings and matters related to their child;
- give or deny their consent prior to the LEA acting with respect to their child;
- disagree with decisions made by the LEA; and
- use IDEA's dispute resolution mechanisms.

In August 2006, regulations guiding the implementation of IDEA were released. In April 2009, Section 300.160 was amended to align IDEA with state flexibility in academic achievement under ESEA as amended by No Child Left Behind (Federal Register, 2007:

These regulations provide States with additional flexibility regarding State, local educational agency (LEA), and school accountability for the achievement of a small group of students with disabilities whose progress is such that, even after receiving appropriate instruction, including special education and related services designed to address the students' individual needs, the students' individualized education program (IEP) teams (IEP Teams) are reasonably certain that the students will not achieve grade-level proficiency within the year covered by the students' IEPs.

These regulations were later amended with the reauthorization of ESEA as the Every Student Succeeds Act (ESSA).

In December 2008, the United States Department of Education (US-DOE) issued nonregulatory guidance on the Part B final supplemental regulations, which implemented IDEA 2004. The supplemental regulations clarify and strengthen Part 300 of the Code of Federal Regulations (34 CFR) in the areas of parental revocation of consent for continued special education and related services; positive efforts to employ and advance qualified individuals with disabilities; nonattorney representation in due process hearings; state monitoring and enforcement; state use of targets and reporting; public attention; and subgrants to local educational agencies (LEAs), base payment adjustments, and reallocation of LEA funds. The federal nonregulatory guidance provides detailed information, including implementation considerations concerning the supplemental regulations. Section I of the nonregulatory guidance should be of considerable interest to school districts and parents as it relates to parental revocation of consent and includes implementation considerations for:

- amendment of records;
- procedures;
- age of majority;
- revocation of consent for a particular service;
- subsequent parent request;
- discipline;
- accommodations; and
- accountability.

On December 12, 2016, the U.S. Department of Education released to the public the final regulations under Part B of IDEA, which promote "equity by targeting widespread disparities in the treatment of students of color with disabilities" (USDE, 2016). The regulations address several issues related to significant disproportionality in the identification, placement, and discipline of students with disabilities based on race or ethnicity and the provision of comprehensive coordinated early intervening services (CCEIS). The regulations establish a common standard for identifying significant disproportionality in representation of students within special education by identification, specific disability category, segregated school settings, and disciplinary actions.

This rule requires school districts where significant disproportionality is found to review their policies, procedures, and practices carefully to identify contributing factors leading to significant disproportionality and determine whether changes are needed. Besides the standard methodology that now applies to children aged 3 to 21, the rule allows for districts identified with significant disproportionality to spend IDEA funds on preschool children and school-aged students with and without disabilities. Previous guidance in this rule limited CCEIS to nondisabled school-aged students.

In Title I Section 601(c)(5) of IDEA, Congress reviews their findings of the almost 30 years' research and states,

The education of children with disabilities can be made more effective by:

1. having high expectations for such children and ensuring their access to the general education curriculum in the regular classroom, to the maximum extent possible;
2. strengthening the role and responsibility of parents and ensuring that families of such children have meaningful opportunities to participate in the education of their children at school and at home;
3. coordinating this title with other local, educational service agency, state, and federal school improvement efforts, including improvement efforts under the Elementary and Secondary Education Act of 1965;
4. providing appropriate special education and related services, and aids and supports in the regular classroom, to such children, whenever appropriate;
5. supporting high-quality, intensive preservice preparation and professional development for all personnel who work with children with disabilities;
6. providing incentives for whole-school approaches, scientifically based early reading programs, positive behavioral interventions and supports, and early intervening services to reduce the need to label children as disabled to address the learning and behavioral needs of such children;
7. focusing resources on teaching and learning while reducing paperwork and requirements that do not assist in improving educational results; and
8. supporting the development and use of technology (5 U.S.C. § 601)."

These eight foci can be seen throughout IDEA and are encompassed in the purpose of the law Section 601(d) (1)(A) to "ensure that all children with disabilities have available to them a free appropriate public education that emphasizes special education and related services designed to meet their unique needs and prepare them for further education, employment, and independent living" (IDEA, 2004).

CONCLUSION

The historical evolution of policies in education and those specifically related to children with disabilities has been a winding and arduous journey. From its inception, public policies have created some challenges in the acceptance of those labeled differently abled, and has demonized their presence as a distraction to the instruction of other students. These early sentiments—despite the onset of compulsory education—often led to the expulsion, exclusion, or segregation of children with disabilities that kept them from receiving a quality public education despite their rights to receive one. The tenacity of advocacy groups, parents, and others to ensure a level playing field brought national attention coupled with a diversity of lawsuits. These efforts have helped to move the needle and ushered in new policies, services, and programs for children with disabilities. Section 504, and the later introduction of the IDEA, opened the door to specific policies and services that all children with disabilities have access to, per federal guidelines. However, despite all the safeguards and rights in place for students with disabilities, their success can be limited only by the expectations of the adults surrounding them. Parents, families, school staff, related service providers, and the states must ensure that students with disabilities are receiving a free and appropriate public education, the same as all students.

REFERENCES

Bohan, C. H., & Null, J. W. (2007). Gender and the evolution of normal school education: A historical analysis of teacher education institutions. *Educational Foundations, 21*(3/4), 3–26. Retrieved from the ERIC database. (No. EJ831197)

Brown v. Board of Education of Topeka, 347 U.S. 483 (May 17, 1954).

Comer, J. P. (2004). *Leave no child behind: Preparing today's youth for tomorrow's world.* New Haven, CN: Yale University Press.

Council Exceptional Children. (n.d.). Retrieved on August 3, 2017 from https://www.cec.sped.org/About-Us/CEC-Milestones

Cremin, L. A. (1970). *American education: The colonial experience, 1607–1783.* New York, NY: Harper & Row.

Education Advocates Coalition (1980). *Report by the Education Advocates Coalition on federal compliance activities to implement the Education for All Handicapped Children Act (PL 94-142).* Retrieved from https://mn.gov/mnddc/parallels2/pdf/80s/80/80-PEA-EAC.pdf

Education for All Handicapped Children Act (EAHCA), Pub. L. No. 94-142, 89 Stat. 773 (1975).

Federal Register. (2007). Vol. 72 No. 67 FR 17748. Retrieved from https://www2.ed.gov/legislation/FedRegister/finrule/2007-2/040907a.html

Honig v. Doe. (1988, June 20). 485 U.S. 305.

Individuals With Disabilities Education Act. (1990). Public Law No. 108-446.

Individuals With Disabilities Education Act. (1997). Public Law No. 108-446.

Individuals With Disabilities Education Improvement Act, 20 U.S.C. § 1400 (2004). Sec.601(d)(1)(A). Public Law No. 108-446.

Iorio, S. H., & Yeager, M. E. (2011, July). *School reform: Past, present and future.* Paper presented at School Reform Strategies: An Interdisciplinary Perspective, Oxford University. Retrieved from http://webs.wichita.edu/

Li, L. (2013, December). *PARC v. Commonwealth of Pennsylvania* and *Mills v. Board of Education, DC.* Retrieved from http://www.rootedinrights.org/15321 -revision-v1/

Mills v. Board of Education of District of Columbia. (1972). 348 F. Supp. 866 (D.D.C.).

Moody, A. (2012, May 3). *The education for all handicapped children act: A faltering step towards integration.* Retrieved August 3, 2017, from http://commons.trincoll. edu/edreform/2012/05/the-education-for-all-handicapped-children-act-a-faltering-step-towards-integration/

PARC v. Commonwealth of Pennsylvania. (1972, October 15). No. 71-42 (E.D. Pa.).

Pierce v. Society of Sisters of the Holy Names of Jesus and Mary. (1925, June 1). 268 U.S. 510.

Saleh, M. (n.d.). *Your child's rights: 6 principles of IDEA.* Retrieved August 3, 2017, from http://www.smartkidswithld.org/getting-help/know-your-childs-rights/ your-childs-rights-6-principles-of-idea/

Sperry, D. J., & Gee, E. G. (1998). *Education law and the public schools: A compendium.* Norwood, MA: Christopher-Gordon.

Turnbull, H. R., III. (1993). *Free appropriate public education: The law and children with disabilities* (4th ed.). Denver, CO: Love.

U.S. Department of Education (USDE). (2016, December 12). *Equity in IDEA: Fact sheet.* Retrieved August 3, 2017, from https://www.ed.gov/news/ press-releases/fact-sheet-equity-idea

U.S. Department of Education, Office for Civil Rights. (2010, August). *Free appropriate public education for students with disabilities: Requirements under section 504 of the Rehabilitation Act of 1973.* Retrieved August 3, 2017, from https://www2. ed.gov/about/offices/list/ocr/docs/edlite-FAPE504.html

Watson, S. (2008, February 13). *How public schools work.* Retrieved June 1, 2011, from http://people.howstuffworks.com/public-schools1.htm

Weber, M. C. (1992). *Special education law and litigation treatise.* Horsham, PA: LRP Publications.

Winzer, Margret, A. (1993). *The history of special education: From isolation to integration.* Washington, DC. Gallaudet Press.

Wisconsin v. Yoder. (1972, May 15). 406 U.S. 205.

Wright, P. (2005). *Individuals with disabilities education act burden of proof: On parents or schools.* Washington: DC: National council on disability. Retrieved from file:///C:/Users/Kristie/Downloads/wright.burdenproof.pdf

Yell, M. L., Rogers, D., & Lodge Rodgers, E. (1998). The legal history of special education. *Remedial & Special Education, 19*(4), 219–228. Retrieved from the MasterFILE Premier database. (No. 1031650)

CHAPTER 2

STRUCTURAL SEGREGATION, DISPROPORTIONATE REPRESENTATION, AND DISABLING ASSUMPTIONS IN SPECIAL EDUCATION

A Black Educator's Narrative

Saran Stewart and David Kennedy
University of the West Indies

ABSTRACT

There is an endemic number of minority students in special education being tracked through, and receiving, remedial education in the United States. However, little has been done to change the system. From a critical race theoretical (CRT) perspective, the purpose of this narrative study is to understand how racism is used as a segregation tool against Black and Hispanic youth in institutions of special education. This narrative study uses the critical reflections and observations of a certified, special education teacher in a midwestern public school district who observed, named, and rejected the inequities forced upon

Untold Narratives, pages 17–31
Copyright © 2018 by Information Age Publishing

minority students in special education. Guided by the literature, this chapter looks at the structural segregation, disproportionate representation, and teachers' disabling assumptions projected in the special education classroom. Situating the data within the context of a CRT frame, the narrative exposes racism at the foundation of an unjust system used to track and remedially educate minority students. The narrative further reveals that the foundation is based on a privileged endeavor encouraged by White interest convergence. Students in special education are slow to exit the special education system in which they are tracked from elementary school to high school. This issue is further exacerbated because students are not largely mainstreamed into general education classrooms. Continued research is necessary to yield affective implications to reduce the number of minority students in special education and equitably matriculate students into mainstream classrooms. This research is critical to unmasking the inequities in special education classrooms as well as revealing the psychosocial costs of teaching while Black in the United States.

There is an endemic number of minority students in special education being tracked through, and receiving, remedial education in the United States (Beratan, 2008; Blanchett, 2006; Harry & Klinger, 2006; Jordan, 2005). The disproportionality of minority students in special education is often viewed as a hegemonic discursive tool, which is propagated by White privilege and racism in the United States (Jordan, 2005). Specifically, this normative type of discourse is "frequently mobilized in order to 'make sense' of the particular differences that some African-American youth exhibit within schools" (Jordan, 2005, p. 129). Accordingly, Beratan (2008) argues that the "disproportionate representation of minority students in special education has long been recognized as a problem in the United States" (p. 337), but little has been done to change the system.

According to the most recent data provided by the U.S. Department of Education (2016, August), approximately 50% of children ages 5–17 identify as White, whereas roughly 14% identify as Black, and 24% as Hispanic (2016, p. iii). However, while only 13% of children and youth ages 3–21 in special education are White, the remaining 87% make up other racial ethnic groups, including 15% Black, 12% Hispanic, and 17% American Indian (U.S. Department of Education, May 2016, p. 97). Underlying this issue is the overwhelming number of referrals by White teachers of students of color to special education settings (Blanchett, 2006; Jordan, 2005).

From a critical race theoretical (CRT) perspective, the purpose of this narrative study is to understand how racism is used as a segregation tool against Black youth in special education classes, and to present the counternarrative of a Black male special educator and one of his African-American students in special education. The research question guiding the study is: How would an analysis of Black boys and men's lives offer a deeper understanding of racialized structural segregation in special education classrooms?

This narrative study uses the critical reflections and observations of a certified, special educator in a midwestern public school district. Additionally, the literature highlights the undergirding issues presented in the narrative: (a) the new legalized form of structural segregation in special education (Blanchett, 2006); (b) the disproportionality of minority students in special education; and (c) teachers' disabling assumptions of minority students. For the purposes of this paper, racism is defined as the individual, structural, political, and social forces that discriminate against people of color (while privileging others) based on the social construction of race by dominant, normative, western ideology (Tatum, 2004).

CRITICAL RACE THEORY

CRT situates racism at the center of the marginalized experiences of Black lives. Coupled with the stratification and structural segregation of special education, CRT provides a lens in which to operationalize White interest convergence through the reflective counternarrative of a Black male, special educator. Interest convergence as explained by Bell (1980) occurs when White people serve to benefit from acts or policies of racial justice. The analysis that follows will show that White interest convergence also occurs when White people benefit at the expense of or even detriment of racial equity and justice.

Although originating out of Critical Legal Studies, CRT has expanded as an analytic standpoint in multiple social science and education disciplines. The following CRT tenets identify and provide an analytic ideology to deconstruct the inequities described in the narrative:

- Racism is endemic to American life and its educational system
- Race neutrality, objectivity, colorblindness, and meritocracy permeate the institutional structure of special education
- Racism is a contributory factor to group advantages and disadvantages
- CRT allows for recognition of experiential knowledge of marginalized people and communities such as Black special educators
- CRT is an interdisciplinary approach adaptive to many contexts, including but not limited to education
- CRT provides a commitment to social justice for the broader goal of ending oppression (adapted from Matsuda, Lawrence, Delgado, & Crenshaw, 1993).

In the case of this study, CRT examines White interest convergence in special education, provides an analysis to uncover racial inequity, and provides storytelling to depict a snapshot of a Black male educator and the life of one of his students to expose "racism in its various permutations" in special education (Ladson-Billings, 2003, p. 9).

THE ROLE OF SPECIAL EDUCATION

Special education services started in the 1970s with the passage of the Education for All Handicapped Children Act (EAHCA), later renamed the Individuals with Disabilities Education Act (IDEA; Vallas, 2009). These laws require each state in the United States to "provide all disabled students with a 'free [and] appropriate public education'" (Vallas, 2009, p. 182). Intellectual disability (ID), previously termed mental retardation (MR), emotional disturbance (ED), and learning disabilities (LD), are the three most prevalent categories that students are diagnosed with in special education (Jordan, 2005).

The role of special education was designed to provide equitable educational opportunities for students with disabilities who were excluded from the education system prior to the 1970s. However, the role of special education has arguably changed to resemble a *de facto* resegregation within schools in which students of color are more likely to be placed in special education than their White counterparts. According to Harry and Klingner (2006), "Race has been an essential ingredient in the construction of American public education, and inevitably, of special education" (p. 10). This reconstructed role essentially resembles a deficit approach that supports the segregation of minority students from White students in American public education. Eitle (2002) argues that "Black students are disproportionately placed in special education programs in order to isolate them from White students in districts that are under court order to desegregate their schools" (p. 582). To further explain, the majority of the teaching population is White, female, and from the middle class, whose previous K–12 experience dictates their current understanding of the classroom. When these teachers see behaviors that do not fit within their own understanding of school and classroom conduct, they are quick to make referrals.

Why do minority students exit special education at much lower rates than their White counterparts, and why do minority special education students have minimal access to the general education curriculum (Blanchett, 2006; Jordan, 2005)? Some scholars have argued that the homogeneity of the U.S. educational policy system continues to privilege dominant groups while further oppressing marginalized groups by placing racialized minority students in special education (Blanchett, 2006; Harry & Klingner, 2006).

STRUCTURAL SEGREGATION IN SPECIAL EDUCATION

A policy such as the No Child Left Behind Act (NCLB) "mandat[ed] nationwide academic achievement assessment of reading and mathematics," as well as the testing of students in special education relying upon individualized education plans (IEP) for appropriate accommodations (Harry & Klingner, 2006, p. 11). Arguably, the NCLB has been heavily criticized for resembling a "teach-to-the-test" syndrome in which students became drones of memorization. Furthermore, there has been little evidence of critical thinking with students measured by the outcomes of standardized tests. This system automatically placed students with disabilities at a disadvantage, embedded in the perceived racial bias in classrooms. More specifically, the Anglo-American culture being the dominant culture in K–12 schools has resulted in a disproportionate number of White teachers in the classroom (Eitle, 2002). Harry and Klingner (2006) note in one of their observations that "the fact that most special education referrals came from White teachers" was an ethnicity issue (p. 50).

Toward this end, scholars have looked at and examined the strong correlation between race, poverty, and special education (Donovan & Cross, 2002), noting the detrimental effects of poverty-based living that exacerbates special education needs, such as lead-based toxins, alcohol use, and maternal depression. Subsequently, researchers such as Dunn (1968) first documented that 60% to 80% of children considered "mentally retarded" were of Afro-American descent and/or of low socioeconomic backgrounds (as cited in Harry & Klingner, 2006). The intersectionality of race and poverty as contributing factors to disproportionality are heavily correlated as dependent variables to this multifaceted problem.

Jordan (2005) explained the detrimental impact of these phenomena by students who attended schools in high-poverty areas and were subjected to "low educational performance expectations, lack of safety, overcrowding and fewer material resources" (p. 135), and as a result were not properly supported to succeed in school. These corollary effects are further examined with the lack of perceived cultural and social capital. In examining these studies, Harry and Klingner (2006) questioned the role that poverty and race played in the negative, stereotypical assumptions of children referred to special education. They further delineated that because of the negative assumptions, White teachers were more likely to refer low-socioeconomic, Black children to special education, further resulting in the disproportionality of minority students in special education.

DISPROPORTIONALITY OF RACIALLY
MINORITIZED STUDENTS

Essentially, "disproportionality exists when students' representation in special education programs... exceeds their proportional enrollment in a school's general population" (Blanchett, 2006, p. 24). In 2010, the general population of Black/African American students (enrolled in school) ages 3–21 made up 14.7% of the total population, but they made up 18.5% of the special education population across all disabilities (U.S. Department of Education, Office of Special Education Programs, 2011).

Similarly, in 2010 the general population of Hispanic/Latino students (enrolled in school) ages 3–21 made up 20.9% (U.S. Census Bureau, Current Population Survey, October 2010), but they made up 21.8% of the special education population across all disabilities (U.S. Department of Education, Office of Special Education Programs, 2011). However, in 2010, White non-Hispanic students ages 3–21 enrolled in school made up 57% of the general population (U.S. Census Bureau, Current Population Survey, October 2010), but only 53% of the total special education population (U.S. Department of Education, Office of Special Education Programs, 2011). Although the percentages are relatively high across all groups, White students are not disproportionately enrolled in special education. Furthermore, according to Klinger et al. (2005), Black students are twice as likely as White students to be labeled as ID, "1.13 times more likely to be labeled as learning disabled, and 1.68 times as likely to be found to have an emotional or behavioral disorder" (as cited in Blanchet, 2006, p. 24).

This history of disproportionality has been traced to the use of intelligence tests and the subsequent labeling of Black children as "mentally retarded" (Jordan, 2005). Harry and Klingner (2006) argued that "the pattern of exclusion introduced by the eugenics movement blended beliefs regarding the genetics of disabilities with beliefs regarding the racial inferiority of non-White peoples" (p. 10). Blanchett (2006) further argued that teachers in racially diverse schools were poorly trained and ill equipped to teach minority students. She continued by stating that "teacher education candidates continued to exit their programs with many of their prior negative perceptions of 'Blackness' and their prejudice, racism, and sense of entitlement regarding White privilege intact and completely unchallenged" (as cited in Gay, 2000). Due to the subjective nature of teacher referrals and evaluations, scholars have argued that "bias or prejudice on the part of teachers is often raised as a potential contributing factor in the disproportionality problem" (Vallas, 2009, p. 188).

TEACHERS' DISABLING ASSUMPTIONS
OF MINORITY STUDENTS

To assess teachers' biases and prejudices toward minority students, it is imperative to look at the role of their referrals and assessments in placing students in special education. Jordan (2005) noted that "the President's Commission on Excellence in Special Education Report (PCESE) reveals that teacher referrals account for more than 80 percent of the students who are identified with high incidence disabilities and placed in special education settings" (p. 130). Harry and Klingner's (2006) study found that "if teachers refer, the clear majority of the children referred will be placed in special education" (p. 97). They also found Black teachers tended to refer fewer students to special education than their White or Hispanic counterparts. The system of assessments and referrals vary by state, district, and even intradistrict. However, Harry and Klingner (2006) stated that students have to meet a certain criteria to be placed in special education. For students with LD, there must be a "presence of discrepancy" between IQ and academic achievement (p. 96).

Students referred for evaluation for ID demonstrate that their overall development is below age norms, and those referred to as having ED demonstrate "that academic achievement must be affected by evident emotional disturbance" (p. 96). For the most part, these referrals are opinionated guesses by nonpsychologists or psychiatrists, and therefore leave room for cultural misunderstanding, implicit and explicit bias, and further acts of prejudice. The lack of a standardized and regulated assessment and referral system continues to exacerbate the inequitable placement of minority students in special education. More specifically, severe or multiple disabilities are typically diagnosed by a medical professional, but high-incidence categories such as learning disorders or emotional disorders are "subjective and can vary greatly across settings and professionals" (Blanchett, 2006, p. 25). These subjective biases lead to issues of race neutrality, color blindness, and meritocracy (Ladson-Billings, 2003), which essentially negate how race may have impacted the educational journey both in terms of opportunities and limitations.

Essentially, Hawley and Nieto (2010) would argue that instructors teach how they themselves had been taught. Therefore, it is assumed that what works for White students works for all students. Jordan (2005) continues this note by stating that "prospective teachers fail to consider the advantages that White people have gained and continue to gain from systems of privilege that subordinate African Americans and others" (p. 140). This belief of meritocracy held by teachers who advocate that all students are granted the same opportunities, and therefore are able to achieve in school the same way, limits their understanding of racial difference and severely restricts the ways of conceptualizing self and other (Jordan, 2005).

These limits and restrictions play into the disabling assumptions that students who reside in dysfunctional homes are of lower socioeconomic backgrounds and are less able to succeed in general classrooms. These assumptions manifest in low expectations of our Black and Hispanic students and in the resulting tracking of students into remedial classes. In our study, we sought to understand how a Black special educator made sense of the issues of structural segregation, disproportionality, and the disabling assumptions of minority students.

NARRATIVE STUDY

Narrative inquiry is both a phenomenon under study and a method of study (Clandinin & Connelly, 2000). It is the way individuals create meaning of their lives as narratives. The procedures for conducting this study consist of focusing on one individual and "gathering data through the collection" (Creswell, 2007, p. 54) of his or her stories and chronicling these experiences to make meaning given the review of literature and the research question: How would an analysis of Black boys' and men's lives offer a deeper understanding of racialized structural segregation in special education classrooms? At the time, David Kennedy, the second author and participant/co-researcher, was a certified, special education teacher in a midwestern school district. The narrative analysis herein originated from a course assignment in 2011, an analysis depicting a collage of comprehensive discussions, conversations, emails, lesson plans, and teaching journals documenting the inequities and subtle microaggressions he faced daily as a special educator in the American K–12 education system.

Originally, this study was intended to be a solo-authored project, in which Kennedy was the participant; however, during the process of analyzing the counternarrative, it was vital to include him as a participant-researcher, to give ownership and in some aspects validation to his lived experiences. In attempting to bracket our biases while validating these accounts, first we independently analyzed all saved emails, documents, and written statements, and then jointly corroborated on those analytic memos. Thereafter, we interviewed his colleagues for corroborating data. From the data, we derived the following themes: structural segregation in special education and providing material hope as alternative success. Tufford and Newman (2010) explain bracketing as a process to describe researchers' attempts, techniques, and methods of controlling for bias, prior experiences, and beliefs about research topics. At the time of the incidences, we both wrote journals and memos and recently revisited those documents to account for our beliefs, feelings, and experiences during the time of the incidences and while writing the article.

At the time, Kennedy was teaching in an urban school district in which 80% of the student population included students of color, but close to 80% of the teaching population was White. The district's report indicated that students in special education made up 11% of the total student population. Of this population in special education, 17% were White, and the remaining 83% were comprised of Black (31.7%), Hispanic (44.4%), Asian (2.9%), and American Indian (0.6%) (DPS, 2013-2014). Kennedy's classroom consisted of students in grades 7 and 8, which included Black and Hispanic students with a range of learning and emotional/behavioral disabilities, as well as students with Down Syndrome and those within the autism spectrum. Pseudonyms are used in what follows for each participant and school district.

STRUCTURAL SEGREGATION IN SPECIAL EDUCATION

The familiar rustle of Kennedy's keys outside the door remind me that he is about to enter. The door opens with a jarring push and he slowly walks in, head bowed low, stacks of paper escaping his right hand's grasp with a tattered backpack hanging on his left shoulder. It was another hard day, I think, which student is it today that has been subjected to the recurring structural insurgencies of White interest-convergence? How many subtle microaggressive statements did he read in his email today? Did they finally terminate him for speaking out against the injustices of minority students in special education programs: lack of resources, lack of advocates, and incorrect Whiteness-as-property, dominant ideological, IEP plans?

"How was your day?" I asked.

He paused, looked up and said, "Not good." I waited for him to continue, "I met with the district head today. He said that Daryl's IEP is 'too political' and that I cannot request a culturally responsive, urban-centered, reevaluation of his disability."

"Why not?" I interrupted.

"Because the IEP is a legally binding document that the district will have to abide by if I have that in it."

"Isn't that the point?"

"Yeah, I know. The head also sat there and instructed me line by line what to delete and rewrite."

"Did you change it?

"No, but I'm tired of this," he said as he held his head in his hands and shook it from left to right.

Daryl and other Black and Hispanic students in Kennedy's class were under constant monitoring from the district: not so they would progress and matriculate out of special education, but so that they would be remedially tracked into further special education classes. These students were more on a school-to-prison pipeline rather than on an education track, as each hour denoted on their IEPs warranted constant supervision and remedial education tasks. After he dropped all the papers on the dining table and sat the backpack on the living room couch, I probed for more answers. He changed out of his work clothes, slumped into the chocolate colored, leather couch next to me with his head bowed low and his shoulders hunched.

As a professionally certified special educator in two states, Kennedy had taught predominantly Black and Hispanic students for 6 years. He spent the first 5 years teaching in the Southeast, in one of the most urban city-centers in the country, and then upon relocating to the Midwest, he taught in another highly populated urban school district. The differences between both state experiences could be attributed to the demographic make-up of the teaching staff in each state. In the Southeast, his team was made up of only Black and Hispanic teachers, whereas in the Midwest, he was the only person of color on the team. He commented about the differences between teaching in these two public school systems:

> Even though I experienced resistance and lowered expectations of success with the students in the South, I was allowed to change that perception ... But here, the current philosophy of a special education center program is to keep these students in a room for an entire day, isolated from the rest of the school, as long as they remain unseen, out of trouble, then the goals of the program have been met. Before I arrived, many of the other teachers didn't know any of the Multi-Intensive Center students and had many misconceptions about who they were and what they were capable of. Now they go on field trips and I make sure they are mainstreamed in the general education classes with the "regular" kids. (Interview with D. Kennedy, May 2011)

In the South, Kennedy incorporated a differentiated, experiential instructional approach that led to increased reading levels and an inclusive IEP. This provided opportunities for mainstreaming or having the students participate in less restrictive learning environments. When he asked to implement these changes with his students in the Midwest, he was met with much resistance.

> I was use to a differentiated system, where I only had students with emotional disabilities, and another teacher taught students with autism, while another taught students who were physically disabled. Here, all the students are lumped into one class. You have students who have been labeled "emotionally disabled," then you have students with Down Syndrome as well as students diagnosed with Asperger's. I keep telling them that this is not how a special ed class should be made up. That make-up only leads to bullying where students with visible disabilities are picked on by students who do not have a visible disability—it's crazy. (Interview with D. Kennedy, May 2011)

The current structure of the district's special education program permeates race-based inequities throughout the students' education. Kennedy explained that all of his students were either Black or Hispanic and that, with the exception of himself, the special education department are composed of White professionals that perpetuate discrimination against students with special needs through a White-interest convergence strategy. Similar to Bell's (1980) illustration of White-interest convergence, this strategy entered into the special education department team meetings, during which the team designed each students' IEP, behavioral management plan, and safety plan to benefit the larger population of students rather than the students with special needs.

The classrooms for the students with special needs were in the rear of the school, directly across from the detention and in-door suspension hall. Without any inclusion classes, the students remained with Kennedy throughout the day except for lunch and physical education (P.E.). Kennedy felt that his students were quarantined and isolated from the general population. To disrupt the status quo, he negotiated with individual teachers to include his students in their classes with the aid of the paraprofessional teacher.

Over time, this pseudo-inclusion program proved to be successful as students were visibly more confident and motivated to learn in those classes. Additionally, Kennedy had more time for planning lessons in the other subject areas he was responsible for. However, the special education department started to reject these new ideas, such as better diversifying the teaching pool to include more Hispanic and Black teachers. When asked how he thought racism played a role in special education, he responded:

> It has been hard to carry out the expectations of this position, because of my disagreement on how the Hispanic and mostly African-American students are being treated. It is clearly obvious to me that there is a disproportionate number of Hispanic and African-American students in the special education system who are being taught to remain in their place and play their roles that are being institutionalized, an indication of what is expected of them in the future to come. (Interview with D. Kennedy, May 2011)

PROVIDING MATERIAL HOPE AS ALTERNATIVE SUCCESS

Duncan-Andrade (2009) described material hope as an aspect of critical hope situated within quality teaching and requiring teachers to "connect schooling to the real material conditions of urban life" (p. 187). Critical hope in this respect rejects the notion of hopelessness and is committed to the ongoing struggle to achieve equitable and optimal learning environments for racially minoritized students. One could argue that in the same way a teacher can provide critical hope, a teacher can also diminish hope, especially when holding disabling assumptions about Black children, as many White teachers do. Daryl was in many ways a "textbook" school-to-prison pipeline Black boy.

Raised by a single parent, Daryl was one of four children living in a Section 8 or low-income, welfare apartment in the urban center. Constantly in detention halls or suspended, he was referred to special education in elementary school and stayed in the multi-intensive program throughout middle school. When he met Kennedy, he was an eighth grader diagnosed with emotional behavioral disorder. He was also the class bully, easily picking on other students with disabilities who were younger. He sought constant attention, whether positive or negative, and needed to be in control of his environment.

In October, during P.E. he was caught showing a BB gun to one of his classmates. The school resource officer arrested and detained him in the juvenile justice system. Upon his return to school, the line between school and prison had blurred. His new IEP detailed half-day attendance at school, in which he would be monitored and assigned a paraprofessional. Prior to the enactment of his new IEP, his mother was called in to meet with the special education team. Half way through the meeting and listening to all the restrictions he would be sentenced to, she broke down crying. She bowed her head low as if she were on trial as a failed mother. She was spoken down to, belittled in many ways, and made to feel powerless and without options. She listened as they lectured her and said that this plan was in his best interest.

Daryl's new IEP detailed that he was not allowed to eat with other students, not even those in his class. If he wanted to go to the restroom, he was to be escorted by the paraprofessional. Kennedy would later attend his court hearing to provide a character testimony and request a revised IEP, which was granted. A modified IEP was agreed upon by the team, which allowed Daryl incrementally increased access to the general student population and reduced supervision. After Kennedy enrolled him in mainstream elective classes such as drama and art, Daryl started to channel his anger through positive mediums such as breakdancing. Recognizing that Daryl liked hip-hop and breakdancing, Kennedy arranged a visit to the nearby university's Black History Month poetry slam, which included a breakdancing competition. Kennedy arranged for Daryl to breakdance, not to compete but to feel valued and receive positive attention. The university students cheered him on, reinforcing the outside validation he searched for at home and at school.

CONCLUSION

This chapter touches the surface of what Black boys and Black male educators experience as structural segregation in special education classrooms.

Specifically illustrating the positioning of the classroom and purposeful separation of special education students from general education students provides a race-based spatial context. The continued tracking of Black males in special education, without hope of being fully mainstreamed; it reinforces White-interest convergence to have Black males outside of honors, advanced placement, and gifted programs. Students in special education are slow to exit the special education system in which they are tracked from elementary school to high school (Blanchett, 2006). In some cases, this prevents special education students from attaining a general education high school diploma. The majority of special education students receive only a completion certificate that cannot be used to enter college (Blanchett, 2006).

The rarity of having a Black male, special educator in the classroom was a counternarrative in itself, especially in a district where African Americans are invisible, silenced, and dehumanized (Bailey, 2016). Witnessing the degradation of his character, expertise, and Blackness as a means of silencing and oppression was arguably a form of hegemonic history-making. Black male special educators, like their students, are treated as expendable. Failure to conform and follow repressive, school-to-prison IEPs can often lead to reprimand, dismissal, and termination of contract (Stewart & Kennedy, 2016). Further research is needed to collectively garner the voices of Black special educators under duress who struggle to truly educate and uplift their students.

Furthermore, the categories in which Black students are overrepresented are in the ID and EH/EBD categories, which are "tantamount to exile from the mainstream of the educational system" (Harry & Klingner, 2006, p. 172). The main sources of inequities stem from "children's opportunities to learn prior to referral, the decision-making processes that led to special education placement, and the quality of the special education experience" (Harry & Klingner, 2006, p. 173). The issue of race and racism that pervades the institution of special education increases barriers to access for minority students in the higher education pipeline. There is a need for further research on the effects of access for minority students matriculating to higher education, and on the implications of racism on the continued disproportionate representation of minority students in special education.

The perpetuation of an unjust system used to track and remedially educate minority students is based on a privileged endeavor encouraged by White interest convergence. Continued research is necessary to yield affective implications to reduce the number of minority students in special education. This research is critical to the discontinuation of institutionalized oppression committed on minority students in special education.

REFERENCES

Bailey, S. R. (2016). *An examination of student and educator experiences in Denver public schools through the voices of African-American teachers and administrators: A qualitative research study.* Retrieved from http://celt.dpsk12.org/wp-content/uploads/2016/08/Dr.-Bailey-Report-FULL.pdf

Bell, D. (1980). Brown v. board of education and the interest-convergence dilemma. *Harvard Law Review, 93*(3), 518–533. Retrieved from the ERIC database. (No. EJ219589).

Beratan, G. (2008). The song remains the same: Transposition and the disproportionate representation of minority students in special education. *Race, Ethnicity and Education, 11*(4), 337–354. Retrieved from the ERIC database. (No. EJ819567).

Blanchett, W. (2006). Disproportionate representation of African American students in special education: Acknowledging the role of White privilege and racism. *Educational Researcher, 35*(6), 24–28. Retrieved from ERIC database. (No. EJ750547).

Denver Public Schools. (2013/2014). *Report of student membership by ethnicity and gender.* Retrieved from http://planning.dpsk12.org/enrollment-reports/standard-reports

Donavan, S., & Cross, C. (2002). *Minority students in special and gifted education.* Washington, DC: National Academy Press.

Duncan-Andrade, J. (2009). Note to educators: Hope required when growing roses in concrete. *Harvard Educational Review, 79*(2), 181–194. Retrieved from the ERIC database. (No. EJ861851)

Dunn, L. (1968). Special education for the mildly retarded: Is much of it justifiable? *Exceptional Children, 35,* 5–22.

Eitle, T. (2002). Special education or racial segregation: Understanding variation in the representation of Black students in educable mentally handicapped programs. *Sociological Quarterly, 43*(4), 575–605. Retrieved from the SocINDEX database. (No. 9372166)

Gay, G. (2000). *Culturally responsive teaching.* New York, NY: Teachers College Press.

Harry, B., & Klingner, J. (2006). *Why are so many minority students in special education: Understanding race and disability in schools.* New York, NY: Teachers College Press.

Hawley, W. D., & Nieto, S. (2010). Another inconvenient truth: Race and ethnicity matter. *Educational Leadership, 68*(3), 66–71. Retrieved from the MasterFILE Premier database. (No. 55114513)

Jordan, K. (2005). Discourses of difference and the overrepresentation of Black students in special education. *Journal of African American History, 90*(1/2), 128–149. Retrieved from the History Reference Center database. (No. 17229271)

Klingner, J., Artiles, A.J., Kozleski, E., Harry, B., Zion, S., Tate, W.,...D. Riley. (2005). Addressing the disproportionate representations of culturally and linguistically diverse students in special education through culturally responsive educational systems. *Education Policy Analysis Archives, 73*(38). Retrieved from http://epaa.asu.edu/epaa/v13n38/

Ladson-Billings, G. (2003). *Critical race theory: Perspectives on the social studies: The profession, policies, and curriculum.* Greenwich, CT: Information Age.

Matsuda, M., Lawrence, C., Delgado, R., & Crenshaw, K. (Eds.). (1993). *Words that wound: Critical race theory, assaultive speech, and the First Amendment.* Boulder, CO: Westview Press.

Stewart, S., & Kennedy, D. (2016). Speaking from the margins: Recounting the experiences of a special educator and his culturally and linguistically diverse students. *Wisconsin English Journal, 58*(2), 176–188. Retrieved from http://journals.sfu.ca/uwmadison/index.php/wej/article/view/887/855

Tatum, B. D. (2004). Family life and school experiences: Factors in the racial identity development of Black youth in White communities. *Journal of Social Issues, 60*(1), 117–135. Retrieved from https://doi.org/10.1111/j.0022-4537.2004.00102.x

U.S. Department of Education. (2016, May). *The condition of education* (Report No. NCES 2016-144). Retrieved from https://nces.ed.gov/pubs2016/2016144.pdf

U.S. Department of Education. (2016, August). *Status and trends in the education of racial and ethnic groups* (Report No. NCES 2016-007). Retrieved from https://nces.ed.gov/pubs2016/2016007.pdf

U.S. Department of Education, Office of Special Education Programs. (2011). *Children with disabilities receiving Special Education Under Part B of the Individuals with Disabilities Education Act* [Data Analysis System (DANS), OMB #1820-0043]. Retrieved from http://www2.ed.gov/about/offices/list/osers/reports.html

Vallas, R. (2009). The disproportionality problem: The overrepresentation of Black students in special education and recommendations for reform. *Virginia Journal of Social Policy and the Law, 17*(1), 181–208. Retrieved from the Academic Search Complete database. (Accession No. 48617745)

PART II

TRANSFORMATIVE FRAMEWORK:
STORIES FROM AFRICAN-AMERICAN MEN

CHAPTER 3

ACCESSING SPECIAL EDUCATION

The Lived Experience of a Black Male with Learning Disabilities

Amar Abbott
Pepperdine University

ABSTRACT

My story is one of navigating the challenges of my educational experiences through the lens of phenomenology (the lived experience). As a Black child in the 1970s and 1980s, I had to access special education in an all-White community when the laws governing special education were new and poorly implemented. By sharing my lived experience of being a Black male with physical and learning disabilities, I hope to provide a counternarrative to the traditional narrative of why Black males are often deemed uneducable. I will describe how I found the human and educational resources to address the barriers I faced along the way. The goal of my story is to empower Black students with disabilities (at all levels of education) and inform the practice of educators who teach them.

Untold Narratives, pages 35–52
Copyright © 2018 by Information Age Publishing

I am a 45-year-old Black man with learning disabilities who has lived through the implementation of laws governing special education and access to accommodations for people with disabilities: The Elementary and Secondary Education Act (ESEA) and the Rehabilitation Act of 1973. I was raised in Napa, California, and educated in a county whose Black student population was less than 1%; fewer than that were Black children enrolled in the county's special education programs. Given the documented history of racism toward Black residents in Napa County, combined with the implementation of the new laws governing educational access, my lived experience as a Black student in special education was challenging, to say the least.

I first received special education services in 1976, when I was a 5-year-old kindergartner. Beginning at that time, and throughout my preK-12 educational experience, I was often the only Black student in my class and, given the rural nature of the Napa community, most of my special educators sorely lacked the necessary pedagogies to provide me with an equitable learning experience. Although the ESEA and the newly minted Rehabilitation Act were in place, the teachers I encountered were not knowledgeable about my disabilities or about how they manifested in educational limitations.

The laws were clear regarding access to an equitable public education, yet I experienced a learning environment where the teachers, and later the guidance counselors, seemed to have few strategies to address my learning challenges and needs. Time and time again, I felt like a guinea pig or a test subject, finding no relief from my struggles in school. My earliest memory was when my 1st-grade teacher discussed with my mother her concerns about my learning, the beginning of my journey in gaining access to an education. In fourth grade, I had a horrendous time with in-class spelling tests, and was growing tired of the endless assessments, learning products, and seemingly untested strategies employed to teach me how to spell. Interestingly, during this time I was introduced to Books on Tape, which became a lifelong successful learning strategy and academic accommodation.

In middle school, my 7th- and 8th-grade experiences were better, once I was introduced to the resource room and a specialist who had knowledge about working with students identified as having special learning needs. In this room, those students who had been identified as needing extra support would work with a teacher on subjects or on other challenging academic tasks. At this period in my life, I was diagnosed with a physical condition that required several surgeries over the next few years. In addition to the challenges of academically accessing my education, I had the additional challenges of physically accessing my learning environment. My high school years remained a struggle academically, but during this time I was introduced to learning strategies designed to address my challenges, and to a great resource specialist who took an interest in helping me succeed.

Upon graduation, while floundering at the local community college where my father worked as a professor, I faced with deciding whether to pursue a college education or make a living doing hands-on work. While attending a private two-year college, I earned a certificate in wet welding (underwater structural welding), and had a successful, well-paid career until a medical disability forced me to leave that chosen occupation. This caused me to return to the local community college in my hometown to pursue an associate's degree, followed by a bachelor's degree in communications with an emphasis in digital media, from California State University, Sacramento, and then a master's degree in educational technologies and leadership, California State University, Eastbay. Currently, I am pursuing my doctorate in learning technologies.

Much like my academic years in Napa, I am still one of a minority of Black students in my cadre, the only one with a verified disability and the only student whose research is related to educational assistive technologies, those designed to enhance and support the learning experiences of people with disabilities. These technologies gave me access to my education and have enhanced and informed my academic and professional practices.

LIVING WITH RACISM IN NAPA

My family moved to the Napa Valley in the early 1970s when my father retired from the Navy. His last duty station was Mare Island Naval Base in Vallejo, 25 minutes from Napa County. Simultaneous to his retirement, my father taught at the local community college, Napa Valley College, where he later became a tenured faculty member. He kept this position for more than 30 years. My father shared many stories about how hard it was for him to buy a house in Napa and how at the time (in the 1970s) there were only two realtors—both of whom were Jewish—who would entertain the idea of selling Napa properties to Black men.

His accounts are corroborated by the findings of Brown's (2015) *"There Are No Black People in Napa": A History of African-Americans in Napa County*, which describes the enforcement of redlining in Napa, a practice of directly or indirectly denying certain populations entrance to select areas based on the desired composition of the neighborhood and the racial ethnicity of those wanting to buy homes in those neighborhoods (p. 96). Napa County redlining covenants were written into mortgage agreements, denying many minority groups access to residential establishments. Brown researched Napa's Declaration of Restrictions dated January 30, 1950, for a specific property, which stated explicitly:

> No persons other than wholly of the White Caucasian Race, shall use, occupy or reside upon any part of, or with and any buildings located in the above described subdivision, except servants or domestics of other races employed by the occupants of any of said lots. (Brown, 2015, p. 108)

This is the historical racial lens that I grew up with in the 1970s, when I was not welcomed in my schools or in my community. Some of my father's stories included racial epithets and other derogatory actions directed toward him and my family (and our home) that were not apparent to me until I was older. My gratitude to my parents for shielding me as much as possible from these heinous acts of racism remains great.

In 1989, my senior year of high school, the Ku Klux Klan was given permission to hold a rally in Napa, which says a lot about Napa's residents and their acceptance of the Klan's long-standing presence in the county. Despite the environment, I, like most Black people, persevered and firmly believe growing up in Napa helped me to be able to successfully navigate the political stream of racism embedded in many systems in the United States. The experience also served me well as I pursued my formal education, especially since laws had been passed that would support my access.

U.S. LAWS THAT GOVERN SPECIAL EDUCATION

According to Martin, "persons with physical and mental disabilities have been the target of discrimination across cultures for thousands of years. On virtually every continent, there are records of isolation, exclusion, and even destruction of persons with disabilities" (Martin, 1996, p. 26). Given this history of discrimination, the U.S. Congress enacted legislation to address the inequities faced by people with disabilities. The Rehabilitation Act of 1973 (later revised to the Americans with Disabilities Act [ADA] of 1990 and amended in 2008) and the Individuals with Disabilities Education Act (IDEA), enacted in 1975, were passed to ensure students with disabilities free access to public education.

Since the passage of these laws, the last 30 years have seen significant changes in the education of people with disabilities that address the inequalities caused by the public education system. Prior to the enactment of these laws, children with disabilities had little exposure to formal school settings primarily because they were deemed "unable to perform academic tasks" (National Association, n.d.), and a special education curriculum meant students would take classes that focused on manual tasks. These experiences often left students with disabilities limited in their ability to work and become contributing members of society.

According to U.S. Department of Justice (2016), the ADA is one of America's most comprehensive pieces of civil rights legislation. The ADA prohibits discrimination against people with disabilities and guarantees that this population will have the same opportunities as everyone else to participate equally in mainstream American life: to enjoy employment opportunities; to purchase goods and services; and to participate in state and local government programs and services. Modeled after the Civil Rights Act of 1964, which prohibits discrimination on the basis of race, color, religion, sex, or national origin, and Section 504 of the Rehabilitation Act of 1973, the ADA is an "equal opportunity" law for people with disabilities (U. S. Department of Justice, 2016).

Since I started my formal education in 1976, these laws should have had a direct impact on my academic path as well as how I would be treated as a student with a disability accessing education, and eventually the world of work. Instead, these laws were poorly enacted, resulting in educational systems and educators who at the time knew little about how students with disabilities should be treated, let alone educated. Given this, most of my academic experiences led me to being a human guinea pig.

A TEST SUBJECT

Memories

The earliest memory of my educational experience was when I was in first grade. It seemed like I was always a step behind the other children. I noticed then, too, that when receiving more direct instruction and understanding what was asked of me, I excelled. I remember a conversation during a parent-teacher conference between my mother and my teacher, Mrs. Henderson, who expressed how I always seemed to be "slower" than the other children in picking up concepts and interacting with the standard curriculum.

My mother's reaction to Mrs. Henderson's report was one of grace and compassion toward me. My mother already knew my limitations and understood as only an involved, loving mother could, that I faced challenges. Looking back on their interaction, there was nothing my teacher revealed that my mother didn't already know. My mother always had great confidence in me, even as a young child. I remember the words that she spoke to Mrs. Henderson, including the tone and tenor: "Amar is an intelligent boy who is just as smart as the other children. Yes, he needs a little more instruction than the other ones, but he's not dumb." My mother stood up for me! Regardless of what society said about her son and his worth, she was very proud of me. In the 1970s in Napa, California, my mother knew the subtext of what was being said and advocated for her son the best way she could.

The Scarlet S (Slow or Stupid or Both)

Starting in the first grade, I was labeled as a slow learner, and that label would be my cross to bear for the rest of my preK-12 academic experiences.

Sometimes it felt as if there was a giant scarlet S for "stupid" sewn on my T-shirts to ensure everyone knew that I was slower and less intelligent than every other child at the school, and to serve as a reminder of my challenges. By 1976, everyone in academia was scrambling to comply with the new disability laws related to educating students with special learning needs; however, teachers were not given appropriate training. Because of the prevailing ignorance regarding teaching students with disabilities, I do not fault Mrs. Henderson or my subsequent educators for their assessments of me or for my inevitable placement in the special education system. Rather, I blame the inadequacies of the educational system for the labels and the emotional scars still carried with me to this day.

While moving through the preK–6 grade levels, I was identified as one of the underachieving children. In the fourth grade, I remember two instances that re-established this fact. The first was the weekly spelling test. It is likely something familiar to those who have been educated in the United States; for me, every spelling test was a grueling, intense, and humiliating experience. Every Monday of every week in the school year, we would get our spelling words for the test the following Friday. My teachers knew that I struggled with spelling, yet they insisted on giving me the spelling test every week with the rest of the class.

Every Friday was a constant, anxiety-ridden, and angry reminder of the "stupid" label worn by me every day, and I always tried to get out of it. Of course I never did. To add insult to injury, my teacher never graded the test; she always had us pass our test to somebody in front of us or behind us to grade it. To combat this, I made a system in my mind to make sure a friend would get my paper, which unfortunately did not always happen. In one instance, I passed my paper to a student who took joy in marking every word I got wrong. He later ridiculed and harassed me and told me how stupid I was each day after that test. Eventually, I got sick of the harassment and decided to do two things to solve the problem: (a) I had a conversation with the boy who teased me about my intelligence, which turned into a very short conversation that we had with our fists behind the baseball backstop, after which he never bothered me again; and (b) I stopped passing my tests to one of my peers and started grading my test myself, alleviating some of my anxiety, but not my anger.

Another instance that reinforced my underachievement was when a 4th-grade teacher told the whole class to pick a book from the shelves available for the class. She broke us up into groups by ability and told us which beginner, intermediate, and advanced books we could read. When she finally got to the beginning readers and I went to go pick my book, I had selected from the wrong section, to which my teacher responded loudly, "No, Amar, that's the wrong stack–it's for immediate readers. You need to go choose from the beginners' book section at the end." I remember it like it was yesterday, hearing her voice from across the room remind me (and my peers) that I was inferior.

In the beginning reading group, there were three of us: the other two were Latino. From my perspective, every classroom experience was an opportunity to emphasize my learning differences, but now looking back through a grown man's eyes, I see that my teachers were ignorant and did not know how their actions made me feel singled out. I'm using the term "ignorant" as the classical definition of one not knowing or understanding their actions. Granted, the laws were implemented 3 years before I started school, so the teachers should have sought out training on how to educate students with disabilities. Instead, I felt that many teachers found implementing a new curriculum a daunting task and maintained the status quo, which was not seeking new knowledge and hoping for the best. As a young Black boy who had always been out of place in his community, their indifference to teaching students like me deemed me substandard.

Endless Testing of New Products

There are many experiences I could share that would further depict the cultural and social environment of my childhood as a Black boy growing up in the Napa Valley educational system, a system that was never designed for people of color, let alone people with disabilities. The system did try to educate me, but did not know how and instead resorted to experimenting with the latest educational ideas about working with a student with disabilities. I was always getting pulled out of class, sometimes two to three times per week, to meet with a resource specialist. Due to being removed from class, I would get unusual looks from the other children upon returning. Some of my classmates would ask me why I was always getting pulled out of the classroom. I would tell them "for testing and I have no idea why."

The resource specialists would perform assessments to try to figure out the best course of action to help me with my academics. I did not fully understand the tests I was taking or the reasoning behind them. All I was told was, "We are going to be running some test to help us better understand how we can help you in class." This was the only explanation I received. I remember one test where there was a projector with a lever that they would flip up and down and show me letters and numbers. There were dozens of tests that used flashcards with numbers, letters, and pictures shown to me session after session. The tests included those for matching things together and putting blocks in certain orders, and the dreaded reading comprehension tests. Meanwhile, I was still in class and had to get other coursework done.

GREAT IDEA!

One day, a teacher came up with a new idea and had someone record a book for me to listen to for better understanding. I don't remember the title, but I remember that it was about small block engines and hot rods used for drag racing in the 1950s. It was the first time I had ever read a book from cover to cover, and it was not some silly beginner's book. It was a subject I was interested in, and for the next two weeks, I couldn't wait to get the audiotape to read the next chapter. After I finished reading the book, I had an oral examination to test what I had learned, and passed with flying colors. There was no question she asked that I could not answer in complete detail. It was the first time in my academic career that I was excited to take a test.

Then my teacher asked me a final question: Did I read the book or just listen to it and remember the details? I looked at her with bewilderment and told her how I listened to the recording and read along with the book. She still did not believe I read the book, even after I reiterated my process to her. To this day, I'm sure she never believed me. However, with this revelation, my educators found a modality that I had academic success with, but I never saw another audiobook until I started purchasing them for myself as an adult.

These experiences are among the reasons that I'm so bitter about my academic foundation: All the experiments and the endless testing resulted in my having to figure out how to best help myself. When there was an experiment that worked, my educators did not explore the implementation of the strategy to help me be successful. I believe this lack of follow through led me to move on to middle school without truly learning how to be a student, how to learn, and, more importantly, how to address my disabilities in an academic environment.

SEVENTH GRADE/EIGHTH GRADE

Resource Room

Fortunately, by the time I reached the seventh and eighth grades, my teachers had a better plan for helping students with disabilities: a resource room to help those with disabilities with their homework both during and after class. By this time, more research had helped to establish some "best practices" to help students like me. I was placed in a specialized English and math curriculum designed to address learning challenges. The resource room had a learning specialist and instructional assistants to help us with homework and answer general questions about the assignments. The system was imperfect because we were still getting pulled out of class and missed learning important subject matter, but it was a step up from grade school where specialized instruction was a nightmare at best.

The negative learning experiences continued throughout junior high. I remember during a mainstreamed Eastern Civilization class, I would often ask to go to the resource room to seek out additional support to comprehend the class content and complete assignments. One time the Civilization instructor said I could not go, citing that I did not complete the last assignment and couldn't go to the resource room until it was completed. I vehemently argued with him, as well as a seventh grader could, telling him that I turned in this assignment and should be allowed to go to get help with the newest assignment. He said "no" and that was the end of the conversation.

I returned to my desk and started working on a timeline assignment that would take me awhile to complete because of my poor spelling ability and slower than average processing speed. I transcribed the dates and locations onto the timeline, a laborious and frustrating task. By the end of the class, I had only two or three items done. That's when a female classmate turned around, looked at my timeline, and stated "I am done with my timeline and you only have two little sections done on yours. What have you been doing all period?" Before I responded, she turned around and started telling her friends how slow I was. Once again, I felt the never-ending harassment of a student with a disability and further ostracized as the only Black student in the class. At that point, I just got my supplies, packed up my books, and left for my next class. I was furious with the teacher and now with my classmate, someone who would have never seen me struggling if I had only been allowed to go to the resource room for support.

When the incident first happened, I told my mother. She was upset, but she turned it into a teachable moment, reiterating what she and my father had told me many times as I was growing up as a Black male in Napa's racist environment:

> You have to know going into any situation dealing with education or any other issue in society, you're going to have to work twice as hard as every other White person you know because of your disability and because you're Black. This is one example of many that you will have to endure in your lifetime.

My parents gave me doses of reality as I was growing up, each one reminding me that to succeed, I would have to be tougher and willing to endure more than any of my White counterparts. That lesson was drilled into my head time and time again and, unfortunately, society has yet to prove my parents wrong.

Physical Disability

Although I had endured enough in my early childhood, life decided that I was not tough enough, so I was diagnosed with a physical disability to go along with my hidden learning disability. The spring of my 8th-grade year,

I started to develop pain in my left hip, which progressively intensified. My mother took me to a doctor who, upon his examination, sent me to get X-rays. The next day the doctor called my mother to bring me down to the hospital to meet with a specialist and do more X-rays. That same afternoon, I was admitted to the hospital and scheduled for further assessment.

The doctors informed my mother and father of the treatment options for my hip, which had slipped into my hip socket. The first option was to put my leg in traction and hope that the tension would gradually pull it out of the socket so they could reset it. The second option was a surgical procedure to physically remove my hip from the socket. I was only 15 years old, and all of the medical decisions were being made by my parents. Once again, nobody, including my parents, told me what was going to happen next and why. My parents decided to do the less invasive traction, a painful process that required a stainless steel 5-inch pin drilled into my shin and a weighted pulley system to start pulling my hip from its socket. When that did not work, I had surgery to repair and to reset my hip.

Following the surgery, I awoke to find myself in a half body cast around my torso and down my entire left leg. Because no one had the forethought to share with me what was going to happen, I was taken completely by surprise. I was in the body cast for approximately five months, and because of the surgery I missed the last part of my 8th-grade year. After the cast was removed, I learned how to walk again, first with crutches and then with a cane. Following my recovery, I had to return to a new school as a high school freshman with new people and a new set of barriers. After that experience, I knew I was tough enough to handle anything. No matter what, I would take on all comers and would fight no matter what challenges life had to present. Whether it was an insult aimed at my race, intelligence, or disability, I knew I was tough enough and had endured enough to handle it.

High School

Upon my return to high school, I was still using crutches and a cane to get around campus, and had already missed the first half of my freshman year. The thing that went through my 16-year-old mind was that I was not only labeled slow and stupid, but people also thought I was retarded because of my crutches. I had a new resource room in high school and some mainstream classes. Despite being a good student and passing all my classes, I was not really enjoying any of them except metal shop and woodshop, which were hands-on. I excelled at these classes because I understood what tasks needed to be accomplished so I could be successful. Consequently, these classes were an important reason why I stayed in school.

During this time, I was fortunate to meet a resource teacher who did not treat me like a guinea pig, but instead introduced new learning strategies, comprehension strategies, and academic skills. This teacher, Mr. Netherton, was different than who I was used to. He explained to me what we were doing, why he was doing it, and why he thought it would work for me before we started doing the work. He taught me educational strategies, and together we would determine whether they benefitted my learning. That was when I started to change my mind about academia due to having an educator who cared so much about me and tried to change my educational experiences.

Because of this dedication, Mr. Netherton would often stay after school to help me learn. He never talked down to me, and always treated me like a student who needed help rather than an uneducable Black student with a disability. I respected and honored his efforts to help me learn, and no matter what he introduced me to, such as a new kind of spelling technique or new computer software, I tried it. At the time, I did not realize the impact he would have on my life. He remains one of my favorite and most respected educators.

Another example of how Mr. Netherton made a positive impact on me was when I had a job in high school umpiring Little League and softball. I enjoyed being behind the plate, calling balls and strikes, and was paid to do so. One evening, a softball coach and I got into a serious disagreement about one of my calls, and I ended up kicking the coach out of the game. To my surprise, the coach was president of the league, and he informed me that we would each have to write up the incident and present it to the league board. The first thoughts that went through my head were that I would have to explain my actions in writing and, of course, I was going to end up sounding like an idiot.

When I told Mr. Netherton what happened, he laughed and said, "I am going to help you out, Amar." As he took me to a computer, he sat down with me and told me to dictate exactly what happened. As I shared my story, he typed it up, and it was the most pleasant experience I ever had with writing. I was articulate and my report was well-written, so I felt pride when I delivered the letter to the board. A week later, the softball league contacted me and said they had made a mistake, and I fortunately didn't have to present my report after all. The remaining 3 years of high school went by at a rapid pace, even if they included summer school to help me make up for missing the first half of my freshman year. As graduation started getting closer, I made plans to attend the local community college where my father taught, despite being apprehensive and not really excited about the prospect of going through more schooling.

Floundering at Community College While Working

In the fall of 1989, I entered Napa Valley College, a campus I knew well. During my first semester, often during the first week, instructors would recognize my name and ask me if I was Ernie Abbott's son. I would answer affirmatively with an eye-roll. When instructors asked me that question, it always seemed that they expected more of me because of my father's brilliance and stature. Yet I knew that because of my learning disability, I was not going to measure up to the idealistic notion that the instructors had about my father. He was one of a handful of Black professors at the college and, as a one of a scant few Black students, his reputation left me doubting my ability to match his intellectual prowess.

I started taking general education classes and pursuing a welding technologies degree, while working at a grocery store on the night crew in a town 30 minutes away, on a good day. There were many times when I rushed from my job to get to school, where the only classes I enjoyed were in welding because the book work was minimal and the hands-on experience was invaluable. Even though I was half asleep from working, I enjoyed welding for the next four hours to progress to the higher levels. However, the learning environments for my general education courses were abysmal, and I ended up on academic probation after my first year.

I still pursued my welding degree as it gave me joy, and one day a gentleman came to the class looking for some welders to help with a big job that needed to stay on schedule. He told the class if we passed our final welding exams, he would hire us and put us to work immediately. For the next two weeks, we all practiced for the test, which I passed with flying colors, and two weeks later I was in a professional shop welding and fitting water filtration systems. That job lasted for three months before I was laid off. I really did not want to go back to school, and did what any welder would do: I found another welding job. That lasted for a year until I was laid off again. I still did not want to go to school, so I went to my next welding job, where I was laid off after another year. This time, I thought about going back to school, but not at a community college. I saw an advertisement for dive school, a video of a man wet welding. After seeing it, I said to myself that I wanted to be a wet welder in the Gulf of Mexico, putting my welding skills to use along with my love of the ocean.

Manual Labor a Must!

The dive school was a year-long program and had three specialties: medtech to become a medic, spectech to do underwater welding inspections, and weldtech to weld metals underwater. Before studying the chosen specialty, students had to complete both traditional lecture and hands-on general education courses teaching them how to be divers. As usual, I suffered through the traditional classes, like physiology. Despite learning the material, I struggled as a student with learning disabilities, and true to form I never asked for help. I was determined to become a diver, and the hands-on courses were where I excelled. My physical disability was not a hindrance in the water, and in the ocean; I jumped and bobbed around as if I were Michael Jordan on the basketball court. I loved the water because it made me feel normal, peaceful, and in a space where I battled one of the harshest environments known to man. After graduating, I headed to Louisiana and the Gulf of Mexico, the mecca of underwater welding.

Should I Stay or Should I Go Now? Career Loss (Loss in General)

I arrived in Louisiana and started working for a huge company. I started as a tender, which meant that I learned about operations on the deck of the ship, supported the welders, and learned other essential job duties. Usually, this stage would last 2 to 3 years, but I finished it in 15 months; after which I became a diver and always had work. Of course, people always talked about my physical disability, which was observable from my limp, but my boss liked my work and sent me on jobs regardless of appearances. I excelled and was promoted up the ranks, making a name for myself. When my boss switched companies, I followed, and within six months, I was a diver for the new company and working regularly in the Gulf of Mexico.

Six months later, I had to take an intense, humiliating, and embarrassing physical, one that ended my diving career. My boss made me a supervisor, and I got to dive sporadically, but I was not happy being offshore. I had a decision to make: should I stay or should I go? For three weeks, I pondered that question. Honestly, I did know what to do, but I knew that I didn't want to stay offshore for the rest of my life. I finally made the decision that would change my life: I decided to go back to school to see what would happen if I applied all my efforts to completing an undergraduate degree.

Academia!?!?

Upon my return to college, I was unsure about my decision because of my past failures. My academic experiences had mostly been miserable, yet there I was attempting to finish my general education courses and welding technology program, and hoping to move on to a 4-year university. As a Black man in Napa, I still faced the discriminatory actions of my living environment and the college I attended, where the overwhelming majority of the faculty, administrators, and staff were White.

Fortunately, a wonderful thing happened in my absence from the educational milieu: Assistive technology (AT), also known as cognitive tools, became available to help students with learning disabilities (LD) be more successful in college. Trainin and Swanson (2005) used the term "cognitive compensations" to describe when students with LD use different cognitive domains to compensate for their disability in an effort to successfully navigate their college courses. The cognitive compensations often result in students learning through the common modalities: auditory, kinesthetic, and visual. The use of cognitive tools assisted students in identifying compensating strategies for their learning challenges.

The most common example of a cognitive tool is a computer application that facilitates the construction of knowledge in any discipline that a college may offer (Jonassen, 1995). The most important aspect of a cognitive tool is that it has the flexibility to give learners the freedom to determine how the tool should be used (Kim & Reeves, 2007). Because of my father, I was a technologist from birth, so my personal background in technology helped me understand how to use cognitive tools to support my academic success in an environment that, at times, I despised.

There were three main assistive technology tools that I began to use successfully— Kurzweil, Dragon NaturallySpeaking, and Inspiration—each helped me to better understand and grasp the material I was learning. Kurzweil is a cognitive tool featuring text-to-speech reading software that helps its users acquire knowledge through different learning modalities, most notably the auditory and visual mode. I started using Kurzweil while reading 180 words per minute; 15 years later I read 400 words per minute. Dragon NaturallySpeaking is a speech-to-text software that allowed me to write all my papers without worrying about spelling and grammar. Inspiration is a mind mapping software to help get ideas organized. To complete written assignments, I would use Inspiration to outline my essays after reading my text using Kurzweil. I would then use Dragon to write and Kurzweil to edit my paper, a process that has remained the same for every paper I have written since finding these tools. Interfacing with technology and seeing success convinced me I could access a college curriculum in a way that had nothing to do with being Black and having a learning disability, but had everything to do with being smart.

Technology helped bring out the best in me academically, yet given all my trials and tribulations over the years, I learned that I have what my father called gumption and what I call heart. Years later, Duckworth (2016) wrote *Grit: The Power of Passion and Perseverance*, and when I read this book, I truly understood the transformation that had taken place in me over the years. As a diver, we had a motto: all go, no quit. All these sources of strength were instilled in me and helped me reach my academic goals. I graduated from Napa Valley College with degrees in liberal arts and welding technology, and transferred to California State University, Sacramento, to pursue my bachelor's degree.

How Did I Get Here?

My first semester at the university was awe inspiring, and I would find myself sitting in the classroom looking around and thinking: How did I get here, somebody screwed up and let me in the door; how much smarter are these people than me? Looking back, the hardest thing I ever did academically was get through community college, and I barely did that. I received my academic accommodations through the Disability Services Office because, as a veteran of special education, I was accustomed to navigating that aspect of my academic life. No longer shy about my disability, I would go to my professors and show them my letter of accommodations outlining what supports I needed both in and out of the classroom.

Even with the long-established mandates granting me access to higher education as a person with a disability, in my new surroundings I still experienced the occasional negative interaction with educators. In one instance, a professor grilled me about the authenticity of my accommodations letter and my need for it. He wanted to verify the letter, and I looked him right in the eye and told him to call the number listed on the letter so we could finish our conversation the next day. I was in disbelief about what happened, especially since every other professor did not have a problem, and in the back of mind my mind wondered if my race played a part in this professor's perception of the validity of my needs. At the following class session, the same instructor told me he would not give me extra time on my exams, a reasonable accommodation I was prescribed. Once I realized the conversation was going nowhere, I reported the issue to the Disability Services Office, who followed up with this professor to ensure he understood the accommodations process and mandates.

This incident took me aback because it seemed that no matter what level of academia I found myself in, I was always going to be the little Black boy who had LD and who was going to be harassed. Except now, I was old enough and intelligent enough to understand the system well enough to be my own advocate. Furthermore, for the first time in my life I knew that I was not the dumbest person in the room, and that epiphany changed the rest of my academic experience. I went on to complete my degree in communications in a year and a half and, being from the San Francisco Bay Area, I knew I had to get my master's degree; so three months later I embarked on my graduate studies.

Déjà Vu, How Did I Get Here?

I started late in the cohort model of my master's program in educational technologies, so my peers had already established bonds and relationships with each other. Many worked in the K-12 environment, while I worked in the community college environment, and once again I was one of just a few students of color in the cohort. I erroneously thought that since my peers were all future educators, we would speak the same language. But we had different perspectives on how technology should be implemented in the learning environment. Perhaps these differences were due to my personal experience being Black, having a learning disability, or being a successful user of AT. Thankfully, by that time I didn't need anybody to help me be academically successful because using technology kept my learning challenges at bay and I knew I was going to be successful.

In the first quarter of my graduate program, I always had that lingering doubt that I was an imposter who never should have been let into any program, let alone a graduate program. This experience was déjà vu, and sometimes I found myself recalling my undergrad experiences. Once again, the demon in the back of my head reared its ugly head, and once again I had an epiphany: even though my peers were smart, I knew I was as smart as or smarter than they were. Recalling my parents' life lessons: I was a Black man in America, so I had to be.

Remembering this, I worked even harder and faster in my studies and graduated from my program in 18 months instead of the standard 24 months. In fact, this was the easiest degree I had earned up to that point, which led me to believe I had overcome much concerning my disabilities and that I had conquered my doubt-inducing demon that questioned my ability to be formally educated. Successfully keeping that demon at bay, 4 years after my graduate program, I enrolled in a doctoral program to pursue a terminal degree in learning technologies.

Terminal Degree

I applied to Pepperdine University's doctoral program as the last stop to "conquering" academia. One of the requirements for being accepted into this program was an interview with the program chair, Dr. Linda Polin, a highly respected academic in her field who used these interviews to see if incoming students were appropriate for the program. My interview was over Skype and I disclosed everything to Dr. Polin about my learning and physical disabilities. We were having a great conversation until she put me on the spot, asking me, "Why do you want to get a doctorate? It's hard work and you have to give up your life. Why do you want to put yourself through that?"

I pondered the question for a minute before I responded and told her I felt like a guinea pig when I went through school and wanted to make sure that the same experience would not happen to other students. The second reason I gave her was wanting to advance my career by earning a terminal degree. But I did not tell her the third and most important reason to me: I wanted my doctorate to show all those people who harassed me, picked on me, and said I was stupid that I was an educable Black man. Yes, one of my major motivating factors for pursuing a doctorate came from spite and the need to prove to those who doubted my intelligence and educability that they were wrong. I know that sounds petty, but I can live with that and am unapologetic about the spite that drives me.

My first semester in the doctoral program was difficult. One of the upperclassmen who was also a graduate assistant told us that a doctoral program is like putting your mouth around the outlet of a fire hydrant and turning it on full blast. The amount of information one is expected to grasp and understand in a timely manner is phenomenal. I had never read so much while simultaneously learning so many different concepts, and found myself overwhelmed with the volume of work demanded of me. The pressure finally came to a head in week five of my first quarter when I had a meltdown and told myself I could not do it. Although I was saddened by the notion of quitting my first term, I knew this was unacceptable because Abbotts don't quit.

That demon reared up in the back of my head again asking me: How did you get here, Black boy, and what are you going to do now? I had to go back to my roots, to my life philosophy of "all go, no quit," and my father's voice in the back of my head saying, "You need to have some gumption, boy!" I also did something that I normally would not have done so readily before: I asked for help. I found the instructors in the program understood much of what I felt and were accommodating to what I needed, attitudes that made all the difference in my learning experience. The demon slowly faded into the background, and I reminded myself that I got to this program on my own merit, I belonged in this program, and nothing or no one could take that away from me.

CONCLUSION

Looking back on my life and my academic career, I cannot separate being a Black male from being a person with disabilities; these two are an integral part of my identity and have shaped me. I have emerged from being a human guinea pig in the K-12 system to earning a terminal degree that allows me to help students like myself thrive in their respective academic pursuits. I must acknowledge the outstanding mentors who have coached and supported me, but they would not have been able to help me if I had not been willing to help myself. Being a commercial diver taught me to keep going and to apply that mindset to the rest of my life. My educational experiences as a community college student with disabilities led me to my current job as a professor of assistive technology at a California community college.

Before I end my story, I'd like to share a quote spoken by Tom Hanks, portraying a softball coach in the movie *A League of Their Own*. When his all-star player was mentally exhausted from trying to compete professionally, he told her, "It's the hard that makes it great!" That's true, but I would like to add that the characteristics that make one worthy of the greatness are one's willingness to dream and persevere, to strive for what others have deemed impossible.

REFERENCES

Brown, A. L. C. (2015). *"There are no Black people in Napa": A history of African Americans in Napa County* (Unpublished master's thesis). Adams State University, Alamosa, CA.

Duckworth, A. (2016). *Grit: The power and passion of perseverance.* New York, NY: Scribner.

Jonassen, D. H. (1995). Computers as cognitive tools: Learning with technology, not from technology. *Journal of Computing in Higher Education, 6*(2), 40–73. Retrieved from Educational Resources Information Center database. (No. EJ506904)

Kim, B., & Reeves, T. C. (2007). Reframing research on learning with technology: In search of the meaning of cognitive tools. *Instructional Science, 35*(3), 207–256. Retrieved from https://doi.org/10.1007/s11251-006-9005-2

Martin, E. W. (1996). The legislative and litigation history of special education. *Future of Children, 6*(1), 25–39. Retrieved from Educational Resources Information Center database. (No. EJ531749)

National Association of Special Education Teachers. (n.d.). *History of special education: The past 60 years.* (PowerPoint). Retrieved April 20, 2017, from http://www.naset.org/

Trainin, G., & Swanson, H. L. (2005). Cognition, metacognition, and achievement of college students with learning disabilities. *Learning Disability Quarterly, 28*(4), 261–272. Retrieved from Educational Resources Information Center database. (No. EJ725678)

U.S. Department of Justice. (2016). *Introduction to the ADA.* Retrieved April 20, 2017, from https://www.ada.gov/ada_intro.htm

CHAPTER 4

A VOICE WITHIN

How Private Speech Continues to Propel One Man to Academic Success

Rev. Russell Ewell II
*Co-Chair of The United Methodist Association
of Ministers With Disabilities*

ABSTRACT

African Americans have found themselves on the receiving end of questions concerning their ability to compete academically with their White contemporaries. Moreover, many have endured the sting of trusted education professionals openly questioning the plausibility of them succeeding in school or contributing to society. Racial bias and poor cultural competency have guided such notions. People with disabilities face similar challenges in that many have been informed they too lack the capacity to compete or even learn at the same level as their abled-bodied counterparts. But one must ask, what are the educational expectations of the individuals who find themselves at the intersection of these two groups? What has openly been said about them, and how has that informed the trajectory of their lives? In this chapter, Russell Ewell reflects on the overwhelming amount of times that this ethos of inability was verbally articulated concerning his future. He also explains how this same ethos guided the pedagogy of those charged with educating

Untold Narratives, pages 53–66
Copyright © 2018 by Information Age Publishing

him. Nevertheless, though these discouraging voices rang loud, he refused to be influenced by these sociocultural learnings. Instead he listened to what theologians refer to as the Holy Spirit, and what educators might call private speech. The author elucidates how this private speech helped to propel him far beyond the early prognosis of educators and his optometrist. They warned his parents that blind students could not succeed in integrated classrooms, and that they shouldn't dream of seeing their son graduate from high school with a diploma.

SOCIOCULTURAL INFLUENCES OR THEOLOGICAL FRAMEWORK

In 1969 at the age of 4, my family and I were parked outside our apartment when someone hit us and drove off. The force of the impact propelled me with such force that I hit my head on the back of the front seat. As a result, my parents were told that I had photophobia and nystagmus. With these vision conditions combined with my low visual acuity, I was diagnosed as being legally blind. Though I was neither diagnosed nor treated for having sustained a head injury, the medical profession now recognizes that any time the head is jarred or injured, that is indeed a head injury.

When it was time for me to begin elementary school, my parents began to research and seek consultation on how to proceed. Unfortunately, we lived in a very modest, nonaffluent area of St. Louis City. This meant that we were within the City of St. Louis Public School District, which was incapable of assisting someone with my disability. I vividly recall sitting outside a room at my local grade school where my parents were meeting with a representative of the school district and my optometrist. This meeting was called by my parents, and was the closest thing to having an official individualized education plan (IEP) consultation that we can recall. This meeting would set the stage for the rest of my life, though no one knew that I was able to hear the conversation. During this conference, my parents were told that blind students could not succeed in integrated classrooms, so they shouldn't dream of one day seeing their son graduate from high school with a diploma. A certificate of completion maybe, but not with a diploma.

Even though St. Louis is home to an extraordinary resource known as the Missouri School for the Blind, we were never told about it. Their suggestion was one of the local schools for "crippled" children. Upon hearing these experts' words, something clicked and I found myself as a child saying in response, "But what does God say?" In other words, I had the choice of not being influenced by these sociocultural learnings. According to McGlonn-Nelson (2005), the Russian psychologist Lev Vygotsky began to contemplate a system to help understand the educational and societal issues of his day. He believed other factors besides biological instincts caused humans to act the way they do. His sociocultural theory concluded that our learning is informed by cultural influences that include peers, adults, institutions, and historical contexts.

Instead, I listened to what theologians would call the Holy Spirit; and what Educators might refer to this as private speech. I have come to understand over the years that this experience and my response formed the substratum of my theological framework, which is to say the overall theological viewpoint that provides a basis or structure for life and thought (McKim, 1996, p. 279). This was the beginning of my questioning the nomenclatures of society. However, at that moment I was questioning the normalcy of low expectations for me as an African-American child with a disability. The word normal has power, and can be weaponized. At this early age, I pushed beyond what was normal or abnormal by understanding that these images expose cultural biases and transform words into value-laden "norms" (Anderson, 2003).

Leaving this meeting, my parents toiled over what to do next. Many days I overheard them pondering and debating how to proceed. One day my father approached me, presented the situation, then asked where would I like to go to school? I told him that I wanted to attend Cote Brilliante Elementary, which was the same school that all my friends from the neighborhood attended and where my older brother had attended. My parents agreed and enrolled me in that public school.

Many of my teachers at Cote Brilliante were not sure how to assist me to be successful in their classrooms. My parents were intentional about meeting with the teachers at the beginning of each term, and would inform them of the challenges I had with seeing printed material and the blackboard. One might surmise that because of the socioeconomic position of this African American community, IEP's in that day were not standard. Incidents of disparities in such communities are not in a vacuum. Here, we often find a high level of poverty, a lack of neighborhood resources, low social capital, and low-quality schools. Since my teachers were not working with an official plan to help me to be successful, my father and older brother became my tutors. Unbeknownst to me at the time, my 5th-grade teacher would put my academic career on a trajectory that would take years for me to overcome.

RELEGATED TO THE PERIPHERY

It was clear from the beginning of the term that this was not going to be a good year. I seemed to be a source of great frustration for my 5th-grade teacher from the very beginning. Just as they'd done every year prior, my parents informed her that I was blind and would need some special attention. Nevertheless, she proceeded as though nothing had been conveyed to her. Each teacher in elementary school taught all the subjects in their classroom. So, when it was time for the reading portion of our class, the teacher would go up and down each row and have students read a passage from a book. When it was my turn, I would respectfully tell her that I could not see the passage well enough to read aloud, but she would have me attempt to read anyway. Since my eyes were unable to focus and because of the way the words registered in my brain, I would stumble and mispronounce words. Often this caused the other children to laugh, which infuriated the teacher because she perceived that I was doing this on purpose.

When she called on me to read something from the board, I would tell her that I could not see it from where I was seated. We were seated in alphabetical order, and that placed me toward the back of the third row. She moved me closer to the board several times, and each time she stated that I was the cause of her seating chart being disrupted. I will never forget an episode when I was seated at the front and was asked to read from the blackboard, and I informed her that I still could not see it. She became enraged, pulled my seat next to her desk, and told me that this would be my permanent place if I remained in her classroom.

In her frustration, she shouted that she was tired of my faking. She then asked, how was I able to walk to school and play with the other children outside during recess if I was unable to see? She believed that I was simply acting out for attention and threatened to send me to the portables, which was where they sent kids who acted out. The portables were temporary structures built to relieve the overcrowded classrooms in the City of St. Louis Public Schools. At this school, no one wanted to be placed there, but when I returned from the Christmas break I was informed that this would be my new classroom. I was aware of the stigma placed on children who found themselves relegated to this class; however, I was unaware of its total implication. It was here that I learned that stigma was a word often used to describe the perceptions that society associates with people who have disabilities.

I would remain warehoused in similar remedial classes for several years. Perhaps it is my mind's way of protecting myself, nevertheless in retrospect my time there seems so insignificant and so inconsequential that I honestly do not remember much about my experiences in the classroom. I do recall the structure of the class in middle school. Here 7th and 8th grade students were in class together. There was a teacher, but there were no lectures; we primarily took tests and played cards all day. I found solace in band and choir classes because I was on equal ground with all the other students. In these classes I learned skills that enabled me to accomplish what was needed to be successful. For example, in marching band, orchestra, and jazz band I would take the sheet music home, place it about an inch in front of my face, and practice and memorize the piece. So, when the band director asked us to play measure 32 to the end but the second time take the coda, I knew exactly what to do because I'd memorized it. And because music is a forward thinking and progressive arena, the teachers here knew of my disability and my technique for learning and supported me 100%.

It was in the music program where I began to develop friendships with students primarily in the gifted and college prep programs. By hanging out with them, I began to realize that there was so much that I'd been missing. Through our casual conversations, I learned what they'd been learning concerning classical authors, important books, influential poems, and the like. In order to engage my friends with confidence, I began to educate myself. I would pick up books from the library, read my older brothers books as well as try to read my fathers college level books.

FREE YOUR MIND AND THE REST WILL FOLLOW

In 1994 the all-female contemporary R&B group En Vogue released a song entitled "Free Your Mind." The hook proclaimed to "Free your mind and the rest will follow." I have extrapolated my own meaning for this segment. When I was in the seventh grade I sang in the Normandy Junior High Choir, and one of our songs would add another layer to my theological framework. It was an adaptation of a poem by Max Ehrmann entitled "Desiderata," which had a narration, read by a graduating eighth grader, and a chorus, which was sung by the seventh graders. I was so struck by the narrator's words that I decided to learn the narration in case it would be sung for my 8th-grade graduation.

I rehearsed the lines all that summer, but another song was chosen for my graduation. Still, a transformative outcome occurred because of my rehearsals. The poem became part of my daily routine and private speech, and I discovered that I have said at least one line of this poem every day from that time until this very moment. I've also come to realize that this poem has informed my life, and I subconsciously have worked to live the ethical life envisioned in this poem.

In my freshman year of high school, I had a revelation brought on by several life events. There were the 2 years of reciting "Desiderata," (Ehrmann, 1927) developing my own education curriculum, cultivating friendships with peers in advanced programs, and realizing that I was just as intelligent as they were. I remember distinctly sitting in class and watching students either complete a worksheet that was supposedly our homework or playing cards. I recall thinking that we had not had one lecture, opened one book, or learned one thing all day. Before I could stop myself, I said out loud, "I don't belong here." After school, I asked to schedule an appointment with the vice principal as soon as possible.

The next day we met and I presented my case. He reviewed my file, which I never knew existed. That's when I learned that I was in the behavioral disabled (BD) program. He informed me that based on my grades, test scores, and classroom behavior, my 5th-grade teacher wrote a report stating that I should be placed in this program. Mind you, when this happened I had no mediation, and my parents do not remember receiving consultation. There was no review, no discussion, and no offered appeal. The vice principal was impressed by the grades and progress reports submitted by my band and choir directors as well as reports concerning my leadership and citizenship.

The vice principal stated that something was not adding up. Nevertheless, because the BD program offered no real academic test scores by which to judge, the only way I could move out of this program would be to test out. He was concerned that I'd not had any courses with academic work since the fifth grade, so he questioned how I would do on such a test. I assured him that I was ready to take the test. The results came back, and I scored at the college prep level in every area but mathematics (much to my father the engineer's chagrin).

In retrospect, I now realize that every child in the BD program had a disability, but the school district did not know how to effectively integrate us into the school setting unless we developed our own plan of escape. I found it interesting that the teachers in the college prep program were much more open to exploring ways of including me and providing accommodations than those who were hired to teach in the program "designed for students with disabilities." The college prep teachers' pedagogy, unlike that of the BD teachers, spoke to their belief that all students had the capacity to learn and excel. This mantra was expressed almost daily, and there was an expectation for the students to live up to their potential. Contrary to the beliefs of the professionals who met with my parents prior to my enrollment in school, I graduated from high school with a diploma. And not a certificate.

IT'S A DIFFERENT WORLD

After graduation, I enrolled in Southern Illinois University at Edwardsville (SIUE) with music as my major. I learned that music was not the major for me after discovering the amount of hours required outside of class in clinics, bands, and practice sessions. With this, I changed my major to TVR Broadcasting. This was prior to the passing of the Americans with Disabilities Act (ADA), so there were no Disabled Students Access Offices at universities to assist students. Furthermore, I was not yet aware of Rehabilitation Services for the Blind (RSB), which is Missouri's vocational rehabilitation (VR) for blind residents. They offered services designed to assist blind students in becoming successfully employed. For college students, this might include tuition assistance, note takers, and adaptive equipment.

In some classes I did well, but I struggled in most. I became frustrated when I recognized that my peers were no smarter than I was. Their advantage was their ability to scan the textbook and see the material on the board, which gave them the ability to answer the professors' questions readily. This gave the appearance that they knew the material when they did not. I did not have this luxury, so my class participation grades suffered as well.

Because SIUE was on a quarter system, it was a 5-year curriculum for students without any challenges. I struggled for 2 full years and 1 year as a part time student. After avoiding it, I found myself in the gatekeeper class, which was taught by the chair of the department. One day he called me into his office and told me that I was failing the class. He proceeded to tell me that not everyone is college material and that I should consider trade school. I discovered years later that he had fed this line to some of the most successful African Americans who graduated from this program.

Now, I don't believe there is anything wrong with trade school, it was just not in my plans. His words almost crushed me because I knew that I'd done all I could. Though I was not aware of what, I knew I needed some assistance to be successful. So, I left school that semester before I was suspended. I moved back to St. Louis and back with my parents and began working in the Dietary Department at Normandy Osteopathic Hospital. The work was steady and provided me with the opportunity to regroup, as it were. After 2 years, I realized that I was making $2 an hour less than someone who'd been there for over 20 years and had reached the highest level of this job's pay scale. Again, I heard that familiar voice which said, "I don't belong here."

In a matter of weeks, I received an unexpected phone call from Sue Matthews, my former academic adviser at SIUE. She informed me that a sweeping civil rights law known as the Americans with Disabilities Act was going to be enacted in a year and that it would change the game for students with disabilities. She informed me that schools would be required to provide reasonable accommodations for students, and she volunteered to begin the Disabled Students Service Department. With that, she asked if I'd be interested in coming back to school. I said yes and made plans to begin that September. Upon my return, everything was quite different. I received great accommodations from the access department. They informed me of VR, and I began working with them. I was introduced to the adaptive technology needed to be successful, and I was introduced to Rita Rice, the director of the local office, who became my mentor and remains one of my biggest supporters.

Because of these new resources, I turned my grade point average around by making all A's my last 2 years as an undergraduate. In addition, I took a position as an intern at SIU as an admissions recruiter. This was only supposed to last one semester; however, I excelled in this role so that the director of recruitment asked me to stay on with his office through my last semester. His intention was to hire me after graduation. A few months prior to my graduation, this department, as well as others, were required to cut their budgets. Not only did this mean they could not hire me, but a senior recruiter was asked to take an early retirement. Still, in 1991 the person who was never supposed to graduate from high school graduated from college with a BS in sociology and a minor in broadcasting.

BACKED INTO A CAREER

Now all my sociology professors, the African-American faculty, staff at SIUE, and my mentors told me that I would do well in the job market after graduation. They assured me that as an African-American male in the social service field, I would be a commodity. So, I left college with high expectations. I applied for several positions, but the first professional position offered to me was at Huddleston Baptist Children's Home in Centralia, Illinois, as a youth and family adviser working to develop life goals and plans with youth who were temporary or permanent wards of the state. Because I did not drive, I moved to Centralia and soon discovered from the local African-American community that my position was coveted because an African American had never held a professional position at this agency.

A little over a year later, a letter from the Divisions of Children and Family Services was sent to all agencies and organizations who received funding from them stating, and I am paraphrasing, that all employees of agencies and organizations who may for any reason have to transport children must have a valid driver's license. Because I did not know my rights and was not aware of the concept of *reasonable accommodations*, we parted ways amicably. I once again found myself in a tough job market.

I applied for professional positions at universities, junior colleges, and social service agencies and organizations. I would receive a call back for interviews and often found myself as one of the finalists. The energy in the room would always be electric and collegial until the minute I told them that I was legally blind and did not drive. At that moment, you could literally feel all the air go out the room, and their attitude would change dramatically. This went on for about a year, and I became so frustrated that I began a letter-writing campaign. I wrote every mayor, senator, congress person, representative, and the president of the United States. Most wrote back acknowledging that they'd received my letter. Others mailed back government resources for people with disabilities. But two letters I received would change the trajectory of my job search. State Senator Carol

Moseley Braun and President William Jefferson Clinton responded, stating that when I found a position that I qualified for, they would send a letter of introduction to the appropriate party.

A few days later I met with my mentor, Rita Rice, and she informed me of a job opening thats requirements read as though I wrote them. The position was for an independent living specialist at Opportunities for Access (OFA) in Mt. Vernon, Illinois, a local center for independent living (CIL). I immediately wrote the senator and president back, informing them that I would be applying for this position. About a week after submitting my application, I received a call from the executive director inviting me to come in for an interview. The interview went exceptionally well, and he told me that they had been interviewing people for two months with no success so would like to offer me the position. As I was leaving he hesitated and then asked, "Who are you?" Bewildered I asked, "What do you mean?" He said, "Your references are exemplary and everyone spoke in glowing terms of you." He then informed me that his office also received letters of recommendation from both Bill Clinton and Senator Braun. Word of my self-advocacy became lore within the disability rights community in the state of Illinois.

During my 2-year tenure at OFA, I developed a deep passion for advocacy, particularly for the poor, the disillusioned, and the disenfranchised. I became a zealot for assisting people with disabilities to recognize their agency and their ability to become full, productive citizens. I left OFA after being poached via phone by Paraquad, the prestigious Center for Independent Living in St. Louis. During my 10 years at Paraquad, I held several positions beginning with minority outreach specialist, and by the end of my time there I had the privilege of being their first director of community relations.

THIS HAS NEVER BEEN DONE BEFORE

Responding to the call to ministry, I applied and was accepted in 2005 into the master's of divinity program at Eden Theological Seminary in St. Louis. Upon receiving confirmation of my acceptance, I contacted Rehabilitation Services for the Blind for their assistance. Eden, like many other seminaries, is a private institution and does not fall under the same guidelines as public institutions do as far as the ADA is concerned. Like Harvard School of Divinity, Princeton School of Theology, and Union Theological Seminary, Eden receives its accreditation from the Association of Theological Schools (ATS). Because of its social consciousness and bent toward justice, the seminary desires to provide services for students with disabilities; however, funding is always cited as an issue.

During my initial meeting with the admissions counselor, she informed me that to her knowledge, there was no record of a blind person successfully graduating from Eden. She was aware of several who'd attempted it, but none had been successful. She assured me that the staff and faculty were open to doing all they could to assist me. The counselor said that there was something about me that led her to believe "we might make history."

Because there was no official office of disability to work through, I had the uncomfortable responsibility of facilitating this relationship. So, prior to the start of every semester, I had to meet with each professor, attempt to explain my disability, make assumptions concerning accommodations I might need, and secure the list of required books so I could scan them into my computer, all the while remaining cognizant of the ego and power that professors possess.

Unfortunately, each course and professor was remarkably different. I had to learn their pedagogy and praxis while learning the ethos of the seminary; the language of the discipline associated with each course; and lastly how to think, write, and speak theologically. Graduate theological institutions seek to offer an academically challenging education while advocating for and embodying justice within their walls, their related religious places of worship, and the public square. The issues and implications here are vast, because seminaries at their core strive to be welcoming places. Nevertheless, students with disabilities often illuminate seminaries' failure to move from hope and theory to practice. Institutions' mission statements often articulate their thoughts about themselves being welcoming; however, everyday situations elucidate the reality. Burch (2003) summarizes this position when he says:

> With some notable exceptions, theological schools have been lagging behind in this welcoming movement. This gap forms the stage for a lack of adequate welcome to persons with disabilities in the life of the churches as well. It is time for theological schools, as leaders in their denominational traditions, to change this reality [by moving this idea of being welcoming] to those with disabilities onto [their] list of top institutional priorities. (p. 24)

Seminary was not only challenging for me as a person with a disability who was blazing that trail, it was also challenging to me as an African American who was not hearing his position being raised in the introductory courses. Seminary was so welcoming to pluralistic thought that the Lordship of Jesus (in this Christian seminary) was being challenged, and I had yet to apprehend the language to articulate my thoughts using the language of the academy. However, this would soon change. I was introduced to the works of Black theologians like James Cone, Howard Thurman, and Cornel West. They provided me with the language to articulate my own theology as my understanding expanded.

Discovering the work of these Black theologians assisted me with the language to express my Blackness; however, I still longed to find myself expressed as a person with a disability in theological discourse. The writings I saw expressed an almost apologetic message, which did not speak to or for me. I came to discover that the authors of these texts were parents and family members of people with disabilities.

In my second year of seminary I ran across Dr. Nancy Eiesland's (1994) seminal book *The Disabled God: Toward a Liberatory Theology of Disability*. She wrote as one who'd been involved in the disability rights movement and who was exploring a liberating theology of disability. I found myself cheering and giving her an imaginary high five just as I did the first time I read a book by James Cone. It was very affirming to find the works of a theologian who was thinking about disability theology in ways like me.

At the start of what was supposed to be my last year of seminary, I once again heard that familiar voice. This time while rereading *The Disabled God*. This time it was instructing me to write a master's thesis based on disability theology. It is important to understand that I was on track to graduate that spring, and deciding to write a thesis at this time meant remaining in seminary for an extra year. One would think that it would be a difficult decision to make, but over the years I have learned to listen to that voice. So I stayed an extra year and wrote a nonrequired thesis entitled "Re-Visioning God and Community: Toward a Practical Theology of Disability."

So, in 2009, the person whose parents were told that he would never graduate from high school with a diploma graduated with his master's degree with honors from an Ivy League school. After graduation, I soon learned why the Spirit directed me to write the thesis. It opened doors for me to sit at tables where I would be the only person there who did not have a PhD. Plus, my thesis has been used as one of the texts for classes on disability theology in seminaries, and it was the genesis for the class on disability justice at Eden Seminary. It continues to open doors of opportunities for me to speak and lecture at conferences across the country.

LIFE EXPERIENCES SHAPE LIFE'S WORK

An individual's understanding of theology, as well as his or her practice of ministry, is informed by one's theological framework. Luck (1999) provides what he calls a broad use of the term "theology." He says that theology refers to "all forms of disciplined study that are carried on by the church, and are used to train church leaders, particularly those who are ordained and that guide church witness and practice" (p. 72). If this is an agreed upon definition, then we must take a serious look at the central theological framework that has informed this: the church's theologies of disability.

Classical theology, which conceived of theology as a kind of objective science of faith, led to centuries of the ecclesia working from an understanding of God and community resulting in the relegation of people with disabilities to the status of the "extreme other" (Bevans, 2002, p. 3). One would anticipate this perspective in that classical theology "was understood as a reflection of faith on the two *loci theologici* (theological sources) of scripture and tradition, the content of which has not and never will be changed and is above culture and historical conditioned expression" (Bevans, 2002, pp. 3–4).

Tragically, this stream of thought has contributed to the creation of barriers, which continue to keep people with disabilities from participating fully in community and in common worship. My work takes on the challenge raised by Eiesland (1994) in her seminal book *The Disabled God: Toward a Liberatory Theology of Disability*. Eiesland invites others to join this dialog contemplating the construction of a liberating theology of disability, and she lays a foundation for a theology that she presumes will speak to persons with physical disabilities. Eiesland understands the difficulties in constructing a theology that works for all disability groups. I, too, understand this daunting task, so I am clear that the theological construct from which I work will speak primarily to those with physical and certain sensory disabilities.

The field of theology has evolved to include groups who approach the theological task using a contextual model for doing theology. With this, we have seen the emergence and development of African theology, Asian American theology, Black theology, feminist theology, queer theology, womanist theology, and others. According to Bevans (2002), contextual theology has radically changed the discipline in that it recognizes "the validity of another *locus theologicus* present in the human experience. Theology that is contextual realizes that culture, history, contemporary thought forms, and so forth are to be considered, along with scripture and tradition, as valid sources for theological expression" (p. 4).

The best practical definition for, or way to explain, *doing theology* was explained to me by the Rev. Dr. Martha Robertson, a professor at Eden. The gist of her elucidations was that doing theology was akin to a cocktail party. Before you enter there were several conversations going on, and when you enter you join in a conversation. Because you bring your authentic self, you don't necessarily change the subject; however, you inform and influence it because of your ethos, your context, your ideals, and even vestiges and vicissitudes.

The importance of my work is that it adds to the conversation around disability theology in an exciting way. It explores the intersectionality of Black liberation theology and the social or minority model of disability theology to continue to develop one stream of disability liberation theology. Furthermore, I hope to construct a methodology for seamlessly integrating a liberating theology of disability into the ethos of congregations. Finally, the expected outcome of such a theology will be to empower people with disabilities to participate fully in their religious settings and to earnestly explore the ways in which they might be called into a lifetime of ministry.

CONCLUSION

My story is not unique. People with disabilities moving through the franchise of public education are faced with many barriers. I spoke with individuals who successfully matriculated through special schools, while pointing to others who should have but did not. One person (we will call him Tim) speaks of how he had an older sister who received her degree in teaching when he was very young. Tim talks about a few of his fellows who were much brighter than he in grade school, but because conventional wisdom and testing relegated them to a certificate curriculum and not a curriculum that led to a high school diploma, they began to regress academically. Though they function at a high level, they now work in sheltered workshops. Tim's sister, in contrast, advocated for him, and he now possesses two master's degrees and has a position where he makes six figures a year.

I am aware of someone else (we will call her Jane) with cerebral palsy, whose parents were told by professionals at St. Louis County Special School District that her test scores showed that she would never pass the placement tests for college. Believing that to be true, her parents, like many other parents of adults with disabilities in the St. Louis area, sent her to a local community college every day. Community college counselors have told me that because these institutions do not turn anyone away from adult education courses, many parents place their adult children with disabilities there because it is cheaper than adult daycare.

After 2 years of taking craft courses, Jane's mother passed, and then it was as though something clicked. She began taking courses that prepared students for college-level curriculums, then college-level courses themselves. She then applied and was admitted. Although it took her 4 years as a full-time student at a 2-year college, she graduated on the dean's list. She transferred to a 4-year university to complete her bachelor's degree. Did I mention that she received a full academic scholarship?

I am aware of many stories like Jane's as well as my own. They have caused me to be an advocate for those who do not have a voice, to work for others until they recognize their agency, and to listen while quietly questioning authority. Living at the intersection of two cultures often marginalized by this *androcentric heteronormative* context helped to form the lens from which I fully operate. As a liberation theologian, I work from a theology of hope and a hermeneutics of suspicion. As a sociologist, I work as a conflict theorist. And while researching for this chapter, I've learned that I draw from critical race theory when critiquing the educational system in America.

AUTHOR BIO

Rev. Harold "Russell" Ewell, II, serves as associate pastor of the Village Church of St. Louis (UMC) and as cochair of the United Methodist Association of Ministers with Disabilities. Russell also has the distinction of being the first blind person to be ordained in the Missouri Conference of the United Methodist Church. For the past 20 years, he has worked in the disability rights' field for several influential agencies and organizations. The subjects of his presentations include disability advocacy and awareness, the disability rights movement, the intersections of religion and disability, and the intersectionality of disability theology and Black liberation theology. When engaging the church and academia on their theology of disability, Russell advocates for a more liberating and inclusive theology. He is passionate about empowering the disenfranchised and assisting all people in realizing their potential, purpose, and worth in the church and in society.

REFERENCES

Anderson, R. (2003). Toward a theology that includes the human experience of disability. In R. Anderson (Ed.), *Graduate theological education and the human experience of disability* (p. 40). Binghamton, NY: Haworth.

Bevans, S. B. (2002). *Models of contextual theology* (Rev., & Exp. ed.). Maryknoll, NY: Orbis Books.

Burch, B. C. (2004). Toward a theology that includes the human experience of disability. In R. Anderson (Ed.), *Graduate theological education and the human experience of disability* (pp. 23–32). Binghamton, NY: Haworth.

Ehrmann, M. (1927). *Go placidly amid the noise and the haste* [Poem]. Terre Haute, IN: Indiana Publishing Company.

Eiesland, N. L. (1994). *The disabled god: Toward a liberatory theology of disability.* Nashville, TN: Abingdon Press

Luck, D. G. (1999). *Why study theology?* St. Louis, MO: Chalice Press.

McGlonn-Nelson, K. (2005). Looking outward: Exploring the intersections of sociocultural theory and gifted education. *Journal of Advanced Academics, 17*(1), 48–55.

McKim, D. K. (1996). Private speech. In *Westminster dictionary of theological terms* (p. 279). Louisville, KY: Westminster John Knox Press.

CHAPTER 5

INSECURITIES OF SPECIAL EDUCATION

What It's Like to Be Black, Male, and Learning Disabled

Ronnie Nelson Sidney, II
Creative Medicine: Healing Through Words, LLC

ABSTRACT

The educational experiences of African-American males in the public school system are wrought with untold challenges for the individual, his community, and society in general. Very seldom do we learn stories of African-American males who were victimized by the system and eventually, through a combination of personal strengths, interpersonal relationships, and chance circumstances beat the odds against them. This chapter tells one such story. Described here are the compelling experiences of an African-American male serviced by a small town special education program that focused on a deficit view of his capabilities. Over time, through a combination of parent advocacy, intercession by a caring teacher, and sheer willpower, the life outcome becomes positive and instructive for others. The dynamic intersection of race, gender, schooling, and parental intervention are demonstrated throughout

Untold Narratives, pages 67–78

this chapter providing resourceful ideas for educators and other advocates interested in developing positive outcomes for African-American males from similar circumstances.

My name is Ronnie Sidney, II, and I was born in Richmond, Virginia, on August 14, 1983, to Gwendolyn and Rev. Dr. Ronnie Sidney, Sr., two hard-working African Americans who were essential to my success. My ethnographic autobiography is written with the perspective of critical race theory (CRT; Artiles, 2011; Blanchett, 2010; Connor, 2006). CRT suggests that all interactions are dynamically impactful on an individual's psychosocial development, either positive or negative. The interactions discussed here particularly influenced my self-esteem as a student, and eventually as a young African-American male placed in special education (Ferri, 2006; Robinson, 2017) growing up in a small town in Virginia.

My father was born and raised in Petersburg, Virginia. He dropped out of high school in the 12th grade, and like many of his peers joined the army in search of the stability of a job and educational opportunities. My mother, a beautiful dark-skinned woman, was born and raised in Dunnsville, Virginia. I watched her work her way from a nurse's aide to a licensed practical nurse. Watching her walk across the stage to earn her degree from Rappahannock Community College was one of my greatest childhood memories.

"Big Ron," my father, was a very accomplished man who went from a high school dropout to earning a doctorate in divinity. My father is also a retired state police officer, and currently works as a bailiff at the courthouse in Tappahannock, Virginia. For over 20 years, my father was also the pastor of Second Baptist Church in Warsaw, Virginia. I spent several days a week in church for one thing or another. Being a preacher's son came with a lot of responsibilities and is a story within itself. I am very thankful for growing up in the church, my experiences instilled a sense of unwavering optimism inside me.

I have one sister, Cherlanda Sidney-Ross, who is 8 years older than me. Cherlanda was the perfect child, excelling academically, athletically, and socially. She was everything I wasn't, which caused some jealousy. She went on to earn her degree in social work from Virginia Commonwealth University. It's ironic that I chose a very similar academic and career path to my sister's.

SETTING THE STAGE

I grew up in a very rural area with very few neighbors. My household included my parents, grandparents, and one sister. I was placed in daycare briefly, but failed to return after a kid pushed me off the top of a slide. After the fall, my grandmother assumed caretaking duties while my parents worked. I stayed under her care until I started kindergarten at Tappahannock Elementary

School in 1988. I don't remember much about kindergarten except for a girl I had a crush on; however, a review of my kindergarten report card gave me some insight into my 5-year-old weaknesses and strengths. The report card noted that I needed to show improvement in the following area: developing left to right progression. But it said that I had accomplished the following: (a) fine muscle development, and (b) works quietly.

I remember having a fondness for one of my kindergarten teachers, Ms. T who was young, attractive, and blonde. On my report card, Ms. T. wrote, "Ronnie tries very hard; however, he is having some difficulty with his work. Please work with him on coloring and writing the numerals 1 through 4." Working quietly has always been challenging for me. Ms. Tignor indicated this when she commented, "He still has much difficulty sitting still and not talking," and "I have enjoyed working with him. He does need to control his talking." Ms. T's comments are indicative of my early challenges in a school environment that was not designed to understand or be responsive to my need to share my stories, be social, and move around. My mother's reply on the report card was the clap back of the year when she wrote, "I think Ronnie is doing quite well being in Kindergarten only 12 weeks with a class of 22 children."

My cousin used to call me "Pluck" because my mom would pluck me upside, every time I did something wrong. My mom used to tell me I would do whatever came to my mind. As a youth, I was very impulsive and spontaneous. I remember pushing my friend off a metal car on the playground and watching him bust his head wide open. I thought I had killed him because of all the blood.

MY EARLY SCHOOLING

In first grade, I had one of the best teachers of all time, her name was Mrs. B. She was one of the few African-American teachers I had as a student in the Essex County Public School system. I remember Mrs. B giving us play money for doing well behaviorally and academically. We could cash the money in for toys and candy. During the middle of the school year she left us to take another job. I was devastated along with the rest of our class. We all loved her, not because she gave us candy, but because she loved us. Mrs. B's positive impact on my life as a student remained with me forever.

The home that I grew up in was on Johnville Road, which is named after the Johnville plantation. I rode the school bus with kids who had the same last name as the family that owned my ancestors. The first time I became aware of my Blackness was in second grade. One of my best friends, who was White, invited me to his birthday party. His cousin, who was in the same grade as us, was on the other side of the yard with some other kids. I thought it was odd that she wasn't playing with us. Some kids came over to where my friend and I were standing and said she wasn't playing with us because I was Black. I remember feeling like I had been punched in the gut. Everything felt so awkward after that moment. I felt like I didn't belong, that my skin color somehow made me unworthy of being at this party. I felt sorry for my friend because people weren't having fun because of me. I just wanted to disappear and teleport home.

According to my father, I was referred to special education in the third grade. I remember hating the third grade. I had two older teachers: one of which was a White male. We butted heads constantly. He had a very authoritarian teaching style, and was easily frustrated by my inability to work quietly. I remember him taking me to another teacher and asking me to do a math problem. I remember doing the problem a different way than I was taught. That moment was the first time in my life I remember feeling alienated. I felt like a sideshow, like a freak. One of my 3rd-grade teachers also suggested to my parents that I take medication. My mother refused to place me on medication, but she and my father felt like special education services would help.

I didn't start feeling the stigma associated with being diagnosed with a learning disability until I entered middle school. I remember going to the school over the summer for special education testing. I sat in the room with just one teacher and completed a series of tests. The ink blot test really caught me off guard. I couldn't believe the teacher was asking me to interpret a bunch of ink on a paper. Some of the tests were easy, others gradually got more difficult. One day the school counselor came over my house to ask my family questions. I was surprised to see her, but the whole visit made me feel special in a way. I later found out she was completing my sociocultural evaluation.

MY SPECIAL EDUCATION EXPERIENCE

My 5th-grade individualized education plan (IEP) indicated that I demonstrated "hyperactive characteristics," concerns were noted in areas of restlessness, distractibility, and impulsivity. One of my teacher's biggest pet peeves was my handwriting. It was one of the most significant difficulties I had, along with poor written expression and organizational skills. The IEP team recommended my desk be placed in an area in the classroom with minimal distractions and use a computer to assist me with organization of written material.

In fifth grade, I was referred to the eye doctor and given glasses. I refused to wear them throughout middle school. I also contracted ringworm, which left a bald spot on the right side of my head. The bald spot made me self-conscious. Some kids would make fun of it, while other's silence made me feel like the elephant in the room. The ring worm really impacted my self-esteem. I didn't like the person I saw in the mirror; I was blind, learning disabled, hyper, skinny, and had big ears. I battled with depression and self-esteem issues until I graduated high school.

For most of my life I felt like a disappointment, especially to my parents. If it wasn't my grades, it was my behavior. I remember my father called me into his room and questioned me about a phone call my mom received the night before. My dad worked nights a lot so he called me in before school. I thought he was just going to lecture me and let me go, but this time was different. He asked me to get on my knees, we held hands and he prayed over me. After we finished, he asked me to get his belt and he whooped my butt.

For a long time, I resented my father; he was the one who signed the papers that allowed the school to place me in the "slow class." My mother was staunchly against labeling me or placing me in special education. She used to tell me the school was putting Black boys in special education for the money. My father felt like it was the only way I could succeed in school. While I was writing the script for "Nelson Beats the Odds," I asked him what classroom interventions worked and he quickly replied, "None." As a parent of a struggling reader, I understand why my father did what he did. He feared me dropping out of school like he did. He feared me becoming a statistic, another body shuffled through the school-to-prison pipeline.

I spent sixth and seventh grade in extreme shame, resenting every day I had to walk into the special education resource room. I lied to my friends about where I was going. Going to class late or early was a daily thing. I had to keep my disability a secret out of fear of being teased for one more thing. The room was big, dark, and at the edge of the building. One of my friends could walk by at any given time and see me sitting in there. I lived with that fear every day, along with the anger associated with a belief that I didn't belong in the class to begin with. I staunchly rejected the learning-disabled label. I felt as if the rest of the class needed this service, not me, because I was smart.

NELSON BEATS THE ODDS

Mrs. T. was my sixth and seventh grade resource teacher. She came into my life at a time when I felt small and needed someone to help me feel big. Mrs. T helped me with my handwriting and organizational skills. Mrs. T encouraged me to take my time when I wrote, and encouraged me to write my homework assignments in a planner. I felt like Mrs. T didn't believe I belonged in her class because she made me made me feel smart and capable. Mrs. T was the champion that I so desperately needed.

Recently, while Mrs. T and I were heading to a book signing for my first graphic novel "Nelson Beats the Odds," she shared a story with me. She remembered a time when I told her I was a ninja. She didn't think anything of it until she read my book and saw the illustration of Nelson in the ninja costume. Nelson is a character I created in my own likeness. I chose the ninja illustration because I love ninjas and felt like it described how I felt trying to hide an already hidden disability. Mrs. T told me she had no idea I was carrying around the special education stigma. To me, the stigma of being placed in special education was greater than my academic and behavioral challenges.

AN INSIDE PERSPECTIVE OF MY SCHOOLING

I worked hard in middle school to prove to my teachers I could do well in the mainstream academic setting. The work in the resource class was extremely easy. At the end of the year, the guidance counselor from the high school helped our grade set class schedules for high school. I sat around a group of friends who weren't in special education and filled out my schedule. They were some of the smartest Black boys in my grade and I wanted to take the classes they had selected. They had no idea I was taking a special education class and that's how I wanted to keep it.

For 2 years I was unable to take a Spanish or French class because it was during the time I had my resource class. It upset me because my friends would tell me how fun it was to learn a foreign language. I had selected algebra I, French and English 8-1, which was a more advanced English class. I remember receiving my schedule in the mail over the summer and the classes I selected were confirmed. Yes! I immediately called my friends on three-way and told them. I was excited, this was the fresh start I needed. But in the back of my mind, I had a feeling something bad would happen.

On the first day of school I was pumped. I was in class with my friends and no one could tell me anything. It wasn't until the last period of the day that my world came crashing down. I was called into the office by my guidance counselor and given a new schedule. Instead of taking algebra I, I was placed in resource math; instead of taking French, I was placed in a developmental reading class. This schedule meant that I would spend most my day in the self-contained special education classroom. I remember the tears swelling up in my eyes to the point I couldn't see. I was angry, depressed, disappointed, heartbroken, sad, enraged, and hopeless. I would have chosen death before I entered the doors of the self-contained special education class.

ARE SELF-CONTAIN CLASSES PRODUCTIVE?

The self-contained room was behind the vocational building between the auto-mechanics and home economics class. It was a very large room with huge windows exposing every special education student in the classroom. There was no way I would be able to keep my secret. Being placed in the self-contained classroom was the final straw, I wanted out of special education. I got off the school bus that day a very broken young man. All I wanted was to be included in classes with my friends.

I remember telling my parents about what happened, threatening never to go back to school. When I was writing the script for "Nelson Beats the Odds," I asked my father how I reacted when I got home, and he said I cried like a baby. I don't remember crying, maybe I suppressed the memory, but every time I remember what happened that day I get emotional. I felt like the school was throwing me in special education because they had given up on me. They didn't believe I could go to college, so they tried to dump me in the self-contained classroom. Not today, not ever, I thought. I grew bitter, full of disdain. If the school doesn't care about me, I don't care about them.

My father came to school the next day and I was removed from the self-contained classes. I remained in special education, but only under advisement. They allowed me an opportunity to take mainstream classes, just not the academically challenging ones I had initially selected. Instead of English 8-1, I was enrolled in the less rigorous English 8-2; Instead of algebra, I was placed in pre-algebra. I wasn't happy with this schedule either. The students who made up the classes I was placed in were all too familiar. The students who were placed in those classes were overwhelmingly Black, poor, and disinterested in school. I was tired of being placed on the lower track, the track where teachers spend more time managing the classes than teaching. The classes where I had to defend my masculinity and try to keep from snapping because someone made fun of my bald spot. I felt like I was being set me up to fail because I would have to be a class clown just to fit in. I didn't want to be a failure.

The one thing I did well was being a class clown. During my 8th-grade prealgebra class, I would throw spit balls, crack jokes, and disrupt class daily. One day my teacher had had enough and told the entire class that none of us were going to college. My initial reaction was shock, then I thought finally, someone had the nerve to say what teachers have been thinking since I was in the third grade. I wasn't surprised he said it because he had threatened to put me out of his class if I didn't straighten up. I figured he thought that way about me and the other Black students, but how dare he discourage the White students; I thought everyone expected them to go to college. In that moment, I made up in my mind that I needed to prove him and everyone who didn't believe in me wrong. I was going to college by any means, I was going to beat the odds.

I TOOK ADVANTAGE OF OPPORTUNITIES

For the next 4 years, I fought for every educational opportunity I got. I re-member taking a career inventory with my special education adviser and was encouraged to work blue-collar jobs. No disrespect to blue-collar workers, but I was not good with my hands. I wanted to be a business man, but according to the assessment I didn't qualify for it. I remained in special education until the end of ninth grade. I felt like it had outlived its usefulness in my life. I rejected the label, classroom, and stigma associated with it. I was determined to show the school that I could succeed in the mainstream classroom.

Transitioning to academically challenging classes featured its own set of challenges. Instead of being one of many Black students in the classroom, I became one of a handful of Black students in the classroom. Everything I did was under surveillance, everything that happened was blamed on me. I had an English teacher deliberately separate the Black males in her class, placing each of us at a separate corner of the classroom. Her attitude to-ward us was dismissive and condescending. I had enough of her, so I or-ganized all the Black males in the classroom and told them we should let the principal know what was going on. I felt like we had an opportunity to get something done because our principal was African American, and he would sympathize with us. Three of my friends backed out of the mission out of fear of retribution. The principal had a talk with my English teacher, which she reminded me of. Speaking up and taking a stand only put the teacher and me further at odds. Nothing changed after the complaint, but I felt like I had to take a stand regardless.

When family comes over now, my mom always tells this funny story about me after I was born. She said I grabbed the scissors the doctor used to cut the umbilical cord and refused to let them go until he dipped my head un-derneath the water. She also told me the nurses in the nursery nicknamed me J.R., a fictional character in the U.S. television series Dallas. She said the nurses would have every baby in the nursery asleep, and then I would wake up crying. My cries then set off a chain reaction, waking up every other baby in the nursery. Once all those babies were up crying, I would go back to sleep. I guess I am a natural born agitator.

AFRICAN AMERICAN MALES LIKE ME
CAN ATTEND COLLEGE

I decided to enroll in community college near the end of my senior year in high school. My GPA upon graduation was a 1.8, my class rank was 73 in a class of 95. I was accepted by two historically Black colleges and universities (HBCU): Norfolk State University and Virginia State University. However I decided not to attend. I felt their academic standards were too low, partly because they accepted me, a student with a 1.8 GPA who didn't take the SAT or ACT. I was also accepted into Old Dominion University, a predominately White institution in Norfolk. A part of me also believed that predominantly White institutions (PWI) were better. I grew up believing the "White man's ice was colder." Proving that I was just as good, if not better, than White students academically was my mission. I wanted to beat them at their own game without any special education accommodations. And I did. I graduated with my bachelor's of science from Old Dominion with a 3.0 GPA, and later earned a master's in social work from Virginia Commonwealth University with a 3.5 GPA.

REFLECTING ON MY PAST

What I found most disturbing about my experience in special education was that I had no idea what my diagnosis was. I knew I had poor handwriting and was hyperactive, but that's about it. My father told me I didn't attend my IEP meetings. I didn't learn that my poor handwriting was associated with a learning issue called dysgraphia until I was featured in a video done by Understood (2017). I found out I was diagnosed as learning disabled after I went to the Essex County School Board and retrieved my files for a paper I was writing at Old Dominion University. I wanted to write a paper about IDEA and desired to learn more about my own experience. I was shocked by how thick the envelope was. I had no idea there was so much information about me that I had not received. No wonder I felt disempowered and hopeless.

I authored and published *Nelson Beats the Odds* after I graduated with my master's in social work degree from Virginia Commonwealth University. I invited my former special education teacher to my graduation because of the pivotal role she played in my development. After graduation, I decided to honor her and six other former teachers at a ceremony at an Essex County School Board meeting. I wanted to thank them for helping me beat the odds. The event became the inspiration behind my book. I wanted to be transparent and use my personal experience as an example for kids struggling in school. Growing up, there were very few children's books that featured African-American teenagers or students with disabilities. I wanted *Nelson Beats the Odds* to be the book I had needed in middle school.

RECOMMENDATION

Based on lived experiences, I believe it is important to provide some recommendations for parents and teachers to support the development of

African-American students' strengths as they prepare for their future. The first recommendation I have for parents and teachers who support the development of African-American males is to take a personal interest in them. Taking interest in a student and finding out who they really are is crucial. Fred Rogers, star of *Mister Rogers' Neighborhood*, said, "Frankly, there isn't anyone you couldn't learn to love once you've heard their story." Each of your students have a unique story, one that deserves to be heard and appreciated.

My second recommendation is advocacy. It's important for parents to assume this role early on. One of the tricky things about advocacy is making sure you're informed. That means researching learning and attention issues; seeking professionals who can help you identify and/or address learning and attention issues; and understanding your child's legal rights. The stigma around learning and attention issues in the African-American community is real. Arming yourself with information can help dispel myths and help children reach their maximum ability.

Teachers need to take an active role in advocating for African-American students, particularly those diagnosed with learning and attention issues. One of the most important things a teacher can do is inform the student about their learning and attention issue. I didn't know what my diagnosis was until I requested my school records while I was in college. Invite kids to their IEP meetings and encourage them to take an active role in their education. Help students develop their voice by first modeling it. This means students need you to stand up for them when conflicts arise with mainstream teachers and administrators. You will build a ton of credibility by showing your students that you have their back. It's easy for students with disabilities to feel like no one believes in them, but it takes just one person who believes in them to help turn their life around.

Helping students get to the point where they begin to identify their goals and become an active participant in the IEP process is the end goal. Kids need to learn to advocate for themselves because no one will be there to hold their hand once you graduate from school. An IEP is more than a document, it is a plan that has the potential to change the trajectory of someone's life. It's imperative that we listen to the goals and objectives expressed by African-American male students and support them in achieving them.

My third recommendation is to help African-American boys see their learning and attention issue as a superpower. Instead of saying learning disability, say different ability. We stigmatize kids inadvertently by the language we use. When I found out I was diagnosed as learning disabled, it felt like someone punched me in the stomach. I rejected the label because I knew I could learn. Many of my former teachers seemed to focus of my deficits instead of my strengths. My 12th-grade English teacher saw my high energy and talking as a strength instead of a deficit. She spoke with me after class one day and recommended I join forensics and debate. Forensics helped me cultivate my public speaking and speech writing abilities at a young age. Now I'm a professional speaker who's getting paid for talking and being energetic.

CONCLUSION

Growing up as an African-American male with learning and attention issues meant I had to become psychologically, emotionally, and physically strong. ADHD and dysgraphia significantly impaired my executive functioning, handwriting, self-regulation, and focus. I refused to wear eyeglasses that corrected my astigmatism because I didn't want to be called names like "Urkel" or "Four-eyes." I learned early on how to defend myself from psychological, emotional, and the physical abuse I suffered at the hands of my African-American male peers. My class time was spent alternating between class clown and church mouse to keep my special education placement a secret. I became a master of putting on masks to hide my vulnerabilities.

In middle school, I suffered from poor self-esteem after contacting a ringworm. I became self-conscious because other students would make fun of me, calling me names like "Plug." Each year I would beg my mother to spend hundreds of dollars on name-brand clothes to deflect attention away from my bald spot. Depression set in during the sixth grade; I was ashamed to talk to anyone about it because I didn't want to look weak. I thought about suicide, but was too afraid to follow through with it. I started bringing a knife to school to defend myself, even fantasized about stabbing a few students to within an inch of their life. I might have followed through with the fantasies had it not been for my former special education teacher, Ruth E. Tobey, entering the picture.

Mrs. Tobey helped me develop the confidence I needed to overcome my personal challenges. Instead of blaming and shaming me like other teachers, Mrs. Tobey would frequently compliment and encourage me. She knew there were things I could improve on—organization, handwriting, my hyperactivity—but she also made me feel like I was smart. Mrs. Tobey never questioned me when I arrived late to her class. I didn't have the heart to tell her I was late because I was embarrassed about being seen in her room.

The impact of being labeled learning disabled taught me how to self-advocate and turn my struggles into my strength. I made it my personal mission to prove to all the teachers and administrators that I wasn't learning disabled. My former teachers' low expectations inspired me to earn my bachelor's and master's degrees. Authoring and publishing *Nelson Beats the Odds* helped me deal with the pain and shame I carried with me for over 20 years. Going from a kid with writing issues to a professional writer is one of my greatest accomplishments. My number one goal is to give African-American males a protagonist they can identify with.

REFERENCES

Artiles, A. J. (2011). Toward an interdisciplinary understanding of educational inequity and difference: The case of the racialization of ability. *Educational Researcher, 40*(9), 431–445.

Blanchett, J. W. (2010). Telling like it is: The role of race, class, & culture in the perpetuation of learning disabilities as a privileged category for the white middle class. *Disability Studies Quarterly, 30*(2). Retrieved from http://dsq-sds.org/article/view/1233/1280

Connor, D. (2006). Michael's story: 'I get into so much trouble just by walking': Narrative knowing and life at the intersections of learning disability, race, and class. *Equity & Excellence in Education, 39,* 154–165.

Ferri, B. A. (2006). Voices in the struggle: In response to 'reining in special education.' *Disability Studies Quarterly, 26*(2), 10–14.

Robinson, S. A. (2017). Me against the world: Autoethnographic poetry. *Disability & Society, 32*(5), 1–5.

Understood for Learning and Attention Issues. (2017). *Video: The journey from a kid with writing issues to a professional writer and speaker.* Retrieved from https://www.understood.org/en/learning-attention-issues/personal-stories/stories-by-adults/video-the-journey-from-a-kid-with-writing-issues-to-a-professional-writer-and-speaker

PART III

TRANSFORMATIVE FRAMEWORK:
STORIES FROM AFRICAN-AMERICAN WOMEN

CHAPTER 6

IT CAN BE DONE

Danyelle Cerillo

ABSTRACT

Many people in the education system may not know how to cope with persons with disabilities. This chapter will explore the endless possibilities of accommodating a student with a disability, and the academic success that can come out of providing appropriate support services. The chapter is a description of my life as an African-American woman who not only received special education services for my blindness, but also turned a "disability" into an ability. Based on my journey and what I have overcome and learned, it is time to stop limiting students' abilities based on their physical or mental limitations. I believe students, parents, and teachers need to realize that "it can be done" for people with disabilities.

My name is Danyelle Cerillo. I was born on January 5, 1991, and at 25 years of age I am the oldest child in my family. I would like to be known as a "normal" young woman. However, a lot of people do not look at me like a normal individual. How is this possible?

Untold Narratives, pages 81–95

HERE IS WHY

I was born with a condition called retinopathy of prematurity (ROP), an eye condition that according to the National Eye Institute's (2014) "affects premature infants weighing about 2¾ pounds (1250 grams) or less." In fact, "about 400–600 infants each year in the U.S. become legally blind from ROP." There are numerous stages that some individuals go through when diagnosed with this disability. These stages determine the severity of the condition. I dealt with Stage 5 ROP. This stage occurs when an infant's retinas detach completely, which in turn leads to complete blindness. The least severe stage of this condition is Stage 1, which causes "mildly abnormal blood vessel growth" but does not affect the vision of premature infants (National Eye Institute, 2014).

Was there another cause to my blindness besides my retinas detaching? Yes, I had to live in an incubator for approximately 3 months. In these incubators, the levels of oxygen were extremely high because they were used to "save the lives of premature infants" (National Eye Institute, 2014). Like other disorders, there were many opportunities to prevent my blindness. Physicians tried to reattach the retinas. Unfortunately, these procedures were not successful. To this day, I cannot see anything.

Despite being the only sightless member of my family, I do not let this keep me from living life to the fullest. My parents believed that it was important for me to be treated equally, along with everyone else in the world. Being totally blind did not mean that I was going to receive special treatment. In addition to being physically disabled, I am an African-American young woman. I did not experience racism during my education or life; I was mainly mistreated because of my blindness. As you will find out in this narrative, people needed to get an understanding about my situation, and to show empathy toward me.

THE BEGINNING OF MY SCHOOLING

As a toddler, I attended the Blind Children's Learning Center (2016), whose mission is to reassure people that "all blind, visually impaired or deaf-blind children deserve services and support to reach their full potential." This organization allows people who are visually impaired to explore life concepts such as how to read Braille, complete household chores, and help in the community. This nonprofit organization also challenges the idea that blindness is a crutch for not only the child, but also everyone in the child's family. Blind Children's Learning Center stresses the importance of independence, self-advocacy, and overcoming obstacles. From ages 2 through 5, I was part of this organization's mission and values.

Here, I explored the concepts of reading and writing letters in Braille and on the computer, cooked different types of food, and participated in other independent living skills. This organization believed in the impact of hands-on learning. This style of learning is beneficial for sightless individuals because it encourages the use of the other senses daily. My parents were encouraged to be a part of this new learning experience during my enrollment at the center. My family and I went through the process of reading and writing in Braille. This prepared my parents and grandmother for the days when I would need help with my homework assignments or labeling household items in Braille.

My parents and grandparents allowed me to practice the skills I learned at the center by using the hands-on learning style to introduce me to household items such as the mop and broom as well as various cooking ingredients. My enrollment at the Blind Children's Learning Center opened my mind to the simple fact that I can do the same tasks as my sighted family members and peers. The only challenge would be adjusting for a task in order for me to have an equal opportunity to learn as much as my sighted peers. My family exhibited the I-can-do attitude and core values of Blind Children's mission as I continued to further my education.

In 1996, I graduated from the Blind Children's Learning Center. It was time for me to use the tools that this agency instilled in me at a public school. For 3 years, I learned about what the world was like by doing hands-on exercises. For instance, I learned to count objects such as blocks or marbles and put them in a bucket. Moreover, there were a plethora of fun activities such as trips to local fairs, visits to local farms to explore the sounds and textures of different farm animals, and exciting adventures grocery shopping. Now that my days of preschool were over, it was time for me to transition to the public school system.

MY TRANSITION AND INCLUSION

Like my sighted peers, I experienced a lot of nervousness about the transition from preschool to kindergarten. I did not interact with a lot of sighted people at Blind Children's, but was placed in a special education class with other people with disabilities upon entering kindergarten. Additionally, I was in a regular class setting with children who did not have disabilities; this concept is called mainstreaming. Why was mainstreaming significant for me during this new transition? It introduced the idea of accepting children with diverse backgrounds and cultures. This is also known as inclusion, to "mix in students with special needs, regardless of the severity of a student's disability or socioeconomic status" (Garwa, 2015). Thus inclusion allows everyone to understand the importance of diversity in the education system.

As I began my journey with the inclusion system at my elementary school, I had to remind myself about the different techniques learned while in preschool. For example, I had to find alternative ways to learn about the alphabet and numbers in my kindergarten class. I could not write and read the alphabet in print, compared to my sighted classmates. As a result, I continued to learn how to read and write the alphabet in Braille by doing reading and writing exercises daily. Additionally, the printed letters of the alphabet were reproduced using sand paper. The sand paper letters gave me a better understanding about how sighted people in my class wrote their letters in print.

While being mainstreamed, I spent the first half of my day in a regular classroom. This allowed me to receive the same education and instruction as my fully abled peers. During the latter part of my day, I would go to a special education class where teachers reinforced all the concepts I had learned with my sighted classmates. This time also gave me numerous opportunities to seek assistance with challenging subjects such as math and English. The processes of inclusion and being mainstreamed occurred from the time I started kindergarten through the fifth grade. Throughout these first six years of my education, there were a lot of positive and negative effects of being in a special education class and a regular classroom. Let me begin with the positive outcomes.

Positive Experiences

The mainstreaming process allowed me to interact with students who were disabled and nondisabled. I believe that it is important for persons with disabilities to have a balance with a diverse community of learners. In other words, if a child with a disability spends 80% of his or her time in a special education class and 20% in a regular classroom, the individual will know how to interact only with persons with disabilities. An equal balance between these communities would allow those with handicaps to spend 50% of their time in the regular classroom and the other 50% in special ed. This would give all individuals the opportunity to learn about interacting with diverse students with various learning styles.

I believe that I developed an equal balance between peers with different learning abilities and my sighted peers while furthering my education. It was extremely difficult for me to socialize with my classmates during my kindergarten and 1st-grade years. I spent most of these years with the people in my special education class. Many of these people were blind like me. I had to learn the importance of asking for assistance when it was needed. For instance, in the special education class, I worked on orienting myself to different parts of my school's campus by using my white cane and sighted assistance. When I practiced orienting myself with the campus and utilizing my mobility during recess, I struggled to navigate and was trapped in a traffic jam! Thus, this experience challenged me to ask both my teachers and peers for navigation help by asking for directions. Additionally, I had many opportunities to practice the sighted guide technique when in an unfamiliar environment.

Many of the students with vision were willing to help me with tasks in and out of the classroom. These positive interactions boosted my confidence as a person who was unable to see. Most of my teachers and peers treated me equally during my first 6 years of being in a public school. Each student learns new ways to communicate with individuals with different disabilities or learning styles. For example, pointing at objects is not helpful to a person who is totally blind. Instead, a person with sight should learn how to provide details, to give the blind individual an idea of where objects are in a room. My peers who communicated to me in a descriptive way developed empathy. Most of the students were open to this concept, but others were not. Even though there were a lot of positive impacts of being mainstreamed, I encountered numerous trials during this new transition.

My Trials

From kindergarten through the fifth grade, there were a lot of students that did not understand why I did not have eyes that see like theirs did. A lot of students in the classroom would say things like, "You shouldn't be in this class because you're not like the rest of us." Moreover, they would even go as far as saying, "Your eyes are strange." Luckily, the insults did not worsen, but they made me experience long-term periods of low self-esteem as an individual who learned differently, even though I could concentrate on my assignments and activities in school.

However, when faced with challenges daily, I could not help but replay the negative words my peers told me in the classroom. I found myself not feeling comfortable attending classes with the other students. The students in the special education class did not judge me based on my capabilities as a peer who was blind. It did not seem right that my handicapped peers and special education teachers were treating me with compassion and respect, while the opposite was happening with the other children. Unfortunately, I had to realize that people will judge others if a specific group does not present suitable qualities.

The positive and negative impacts of being mainstreamed allowed me to experience the highs and lows of being a sightless person in a sighted world. During my years of kindergarten through the third grade, I believe the students and teachers were open to the opportunity of having a visually impaired student in their classroom. Everyone was willing to assist me with tasks such as art projects and guide me on class field trips. On the other hand, the 4th and 5th grade years were the start of the period of low self-esteem.

I always wanted to know what changed during these 2 years. I was the same individual who the sighted students helped in the third grade, but what changed? As stated before, some students were not willing to accept the fact that I was totally blind and needed accommodations on certain assignments in and out of school. The fourth and fifth grades were the most challenging years emotionally and socially during my elementary school education. Was there any hope for my future? Would I be able to overcome the adversity that was constantly thrown in my direction?

I Remained Hopeful: My Disability Didn't Stop Me!

The answers to these questions were "yes." There was hope for my future. During my first 6 years in the public school system, I was at Nuffer Elementary, located in the Norwalk, California, School District, which introduced me to the concept of inclusion within a community of students with different learning styles (i.e., disabled and fully abled). The second transition in my education occurred during the summer of 2002 as I completed the fifth grade and transitioned to Emery Elementary School, which taught children who were in kindergarten through the sixth grade. While beginning my sixth-grade education at Emery, I had to keep a couple things in mind. To begin, I transitioned to a different California school district. Emery was in the Buena Park School District. In addition to transitioning to a new school, I was the only visually impaired student in the sixth grade.

How Did I Feel About This New Change in My Life?

I believe that this was a significant transition for me, my peers, and my teachers. A plethora of changes occurred during the sixth grade through my senior year of high school. Let's start with the sixth grade, where I had the opportunity to receive the same lesson plans as my peers who had their vision. I stayed in the same classroom all day without going to a special education. This had more positive effects than negative ones. For instance, many students and staff were not sure how to approach a sightless individual. This gave me numerous opportunities to educate people about blindness. I did this by putting the names of my classmates in Braille. This gave all my peers the chance to learn about the importance of Braille and how this writing system was used in my life.

Not only did I have an opportunity to teach my peers and school staff about Braille, but also some of my friends learned about how to orientate themselves to their environments without sight. While I walked around the campus of Emery Elementary, many students from all grade levels would examine the way I oriented myself, navigated, and adapted to my environment. Rather than explaining the purpose of my cane, I invited students to walk around a small area with their eyes closed and with my cane. Many students described their experiences as beneficial. Students concluded that I was still able to adapt to my surroundings, even though I did not have sight. As a result, a lot of students were not afraid to ask me questions about living life as a blind person. Although I had many positive outcomes of being the only sightless individual at Emery, there were some challenges that had to be faced.

Still an Uphill Battle

In the classroom, my schoolwork and exams took a long time for me to finish, as compared to my sighted peers. Math, science projects, and history reports had to be completed in Braille or on the computer. As a sixth grader, I was still learning how to research numerous topics on the computer and faced challenges. Still, my challenges forced my teacher and I to effectively communicate and work together on different assignments. Additionally, I worked one-on-one with an aide during math time and a teacher of the visually impaired with art projects and other subjects. I overcame my 6th-grade year at Emery by receiving honor roll awards and accomplishing my goals during this new transition. Once the sixth grade concluded, I continued my education at Buena Park Junior High. My junior high years presented opportunities to educate all students and staff about special accommodations for persons with disabilities. How did these accommodations begin?

JUNIOR HIGH

New Opportunities

These special accommodations began as I oriented myself to the new campus. I noticed that all the classrooms and bathrooms did not have Braille signs near their buildings. According to the Americans with Disabilities Act (ADA) signs need to be used for "interior rooms or spaces where the sign is not likely to change over time" (ADA Central, 2016). What changes did my junior high school make? The solution was simple. My orientation and mobility instructor and I spoke to the Buena Park School District about putting ADA compliance signs near all the classrooms and bathrooms. All of this took place before I began my 7th- and 8th-grade years.

I believe that telling the school district about having these ADA compliance signs gave everyone a better understanding about accommodating someone who is visually impaired. Many students and staff were amazed by the way I navigated around the campus with the signs as my guide. This allowed me to educate everyone about the importance of making sure people who were blind felt safe as they orientated themselves with and navigated around the campus. Since I was navigating to six different classrooms like my sighted peers, it was important for me to memorize every part of the campus.

I would spend hours walking the routes to my classes before each school year. Even when periods of construction occurred on the campus, I still managed to get to all my classes safely throughout my 7th- and 8th-grade years. I knew that challenges were always going to arise, such as if teachers did not know how to treat a sightless individual in their classes. During my 7th-grade year, I had an instance of discrimination in one of my classes.

Academic Discrimination Didn't Stop Me

Ever since the sixth grade, I had met with my teachers before the school year began. A teacher of the visually impaired, a mobility specialist, a teacher's aide, my mom, and I would have an informal conference with my teachers to discuss expectations for me to succeed in the classroom. During my first year in junior high, I had a chance to talk to all my teachers about how to acknowledge and accommodate someone who was blind. Everyone was excited about this new opportunity. My mom and I encouraged my teachers to ask me questions throughout the school year if any challenges were faced. Most of my teachers did an excellent job making sure my homework and classwork assignments were placed in a box a week in advance to be transcribed into Braille.

Unfortunately, my world history teacher did not comply with my needed accommodation. During my first two months of taking this class, my teacher constantly handed me print assignments and expected me to turn in my work the next day like my sighted classmates. My aide, my teacher of the visually impaired, and my mom were not happy with the mistreatment I was receiving from this specific instructor. In addition, I was falling behind in world history because I was getting assignments in Braille a week after they were due. On the contrary, I pushed through the first quarter of my 7th-grade year amid this hardship. Before the second quarter began, my mom and the teacher of the visually impaired made the decision for me to transfer to another world history instructor.

We had another informal conference with the new instructor. He was open to trying his best to make sure I was involved in the classroom alongside my sighted peers. He understood that my success in his course was equally important. This example of discrimination in the seventh grade taught me that not all my instructors were willing to change their teaching styles to accommodate a student with a visual impairment. Keep in mind, this discrimination was based only on my disability. Thankfully, I did not get mistreated because of my race or gender. I did not have any issues of discrimination during my 8th-grade year. When I left Buena Park Junior High, the students and faculty were grateful that they had an opportunity to be around a person who had a disability. Throughout the years, other blind children who attended the junior high received appropriate accommodations. Once my years at Buena Park Junior High concluded, it was time for me to experience high school.

MY HIGH SCHOOL EXPERIENCE

Leading the Way

I attended Sunny Hills High School in Fullerton, California. According to an article about me in the *Orange County Register*, "Cerillo, 18, was the first totally blind student in recent memory to complete all four years at the west Fullerton high school." This was a major accomplishment for me because a lot of students and faculty members were willing and ready to accept a sightless individual on their campus. Many schools are not open to the challenge of accommodating a student who is visually impaired, but this was not the case when I attended Sunny Hills High School.

Throughout my years of high school, I continued to have informal conferences with my teachers before the start of each school year. In addition, I made it an essential duty to talk to my instructors daily. It was important for them to have that one-on-one relationship with me since many did not have experience with teaching someone totally blind. Thus, my high school teachers appreciated this one-on-one time with me because it gave them the reassurance it was acceptable to ask me questions if they were unsure of a subject or how I would be able to complete an assignment or project.

Most of my teachers were open to accommodating me. I rarely experienced discrimination and mistreatment during my high school years. Math was always a difficult subject for me during my educational career. I had to work with an aide in my math classes to better understand the visual content on the board. My math teachers would have to constantly be reminded to dictate the content they wrote on the board. If my aide was unable to come to my math classes, I had to rely on my teachers to describe every problem or drawing to me. If I still did not understand the topics that were being discussed, I stayed after school to have more one-on-one time with my math instructors. This allowed them to better understand my frustrations and be creative in their teaching.

Not only did my teachers appreciate me sacrificing my time, they were also open to the exciting opportunities to have a blind person in their courses. For instance, during my entire high school career, I participated in two women's choirs. Before my freshman year, my choir instructor asked a simple question: "How is Danyelle in regards to learning music?" Without hesitation, my mom explained to my instructor that I had the ability to memorize songs after constant repetition. During my 4-year journey in the choir classes, my instructor was impressed by my ability to recognize different musical notes, time signatures, and types of musical chords. Before I graduated, my instructor stated, "She brought a new facet of loving and teaching music into my life, and I know the other students learned a lot" (Giasone, 2009).

This is one of the many examples of how my instructors were open to having a visually impaired student in their classes. In June 2009, I graduated from Sunny Hills High School with high honors. This was a significant accomplishment for me since I was the first blind person to graduate from this school. Moreover, this accomplishment laid a foundation for other sightless individuals to attend this school. I then made the decision to start my college education at the University of Arizona in order to put all the skills of independence that I had gained over the years to the test.

GIRLS LIKE ME DO ATTEND COLLEGE

University of Arizona

When I made the decision to attend an out-of-state college, I knew more challenges would be encountered both on and off campus. Before my first year on this campus, I hoped that I would receive an orientation to parts of the campus, like I did while in California. However, I realized that this campus was twice as big as my high school. Therefore, I could only get oriented to the main buildings before I started classes in the fall of 2009. Even though I did not receive an orientation to the entire college campus, it was important for me to know where all the students met daily.

As I began my education at the University of Arizona, I had to constantly communicate with my instructors. Every semester, I made it a priority to introduce myself to my professors on the first day of each class. I wanted each professor to know who I was and how they could accommodate me based on my disability. Additionally, I made it a priority to attend office hours with my instructors if I did not understand a topic in class.

These priorities allowed me to make a smooth transition from high school to college. Moreover, I had to stay in touch with the university's disability resource center (DRC). The DRC was a place where materials for my classes were embossed into Braille or converted into a Microsoft Word or pdf document. I was also able to purchase my textbooks from the university bookstore before my classes began. The DRC had ways to scan print textbooks into Word and pdf documents. This allowed me to carry my textbooks on my computer without worrying about carrying hard copies of the textbooks.

Not only did I have to learn how to adapt to not having my books in Braille, I had the opportunity to take my exams in the testing center. This was important because I could take my exams for an extended amount of time. In addition, I had to learn how to do most of my work online. I was not used to this, since a lot of my materials were produced in Braille from kindergarten through 12th grade. The DRC allowed me to adjust to everything being digital. Many staff could teach me how to use websites such as Desire to Learn (D2L) and Dropbox to make sure my assignments were turned in on time. As I maintained communication with the DRC, my professors, and my classmates, I could adjust to going to my college courses from 2009 to 2013. Moreover, I had to learn how to adjust to life outside of the classroom. What did this look like during those 4 years out of state?

Academically Independent

I had to transition from my parents doing tasks for me to doing household chores and other tasks on my own. My parents prepared me for this moment. For instance, I lived in the college dorms for 3 years, which forced me to communicate with my roommates if we had any disagreements or if I just needed support. I also had to initiate conversations about clubs and recreational activities on campus as it was essential for me to be involved in extracurricular activities.

After the 3 years in the dorms, I transitioned to an off-campus apartment. I believe that this was a meaningful transition because it was my last year as a student at this university. Additionally, having my own apartment would prepare me for life afterwards. When I had my apartment, I had to consider multiple factors. How was I going to get to and from school? Were there apartments that were fully furnished? What stores, restaurants, or places of recreation were near the complex? During the last two months of my junior year of college, I worked on finding answers to my questions.

My parents and I even went to different apartment complexes near the university. When I made my decision about the type of apartment I desired, it was time to make the necessary adjustments to manage the apartment. My parents and I had to label all the appliances in Braille or with tactile dots.

They also had to orient me to various parts of the complex since I would be living there for the entire school year. Once these adjustments were made, I could take care of myself just like my sighted peers.

Attending the University of Arizona was a challenge that I was willing to face after high school ended. Why was I ready to take on this challenge? As mentioned previously, I wanted to utilize all the skills that my family, teachers, and organizations for the blind taught me. Going to an out-of-state school was not going to be easy, but it was what I desired. I prepared for this challenge by attending a transitional program for young adults at an organization called the Junior Blind of America. This program was called the Student Transition and Enrichment Program (STEP; n.d.), whose purpose was "to help teens and young adults identify areas of career interest and successfully transition to independent living, college, or the workforce."

This program prepared me for living with roommates, maintaining punctuality for important meetings, managing an apartment, and other parts of daily living. If I had not attended this program before my undergraduate years, I would not have had the confidence to go to another state by myself and would have had trouble advocating for myself. The STEP program gave me three weeks to prepare for the 4 years I would be in Tucson. This type of preparation allowed me to become independent, attend an out-of-state school, and graduate with my bachelor's in linguistics and a minor in Spanish.

ACCOMMODATIONS, ADAPTABLE, AND ACCOMPLISHMENTS

All my accomplishments in the educational system would not have been possible unless special accommodations had been made. These accommodations were significant, they are "changes that will enable an individual to do a task" (DelPo, 2017). These changes allow an equal amount of treatment for individuals with disabilities. It is important for individuals with disabilities to not be considered inferior because of their physical or mental limitations. Special accommodations occur only if those with a disability state their needs.

I have dealt with special accommodations in the educational system for many years. Most of my instructors were willing to make meaningful changes for me to pass their classes. However, there were some instructors that were not willing to accept the challenge of having a blind student in their class. How did I manage the people who did not want to utilize the various special accommodations for a person who has a handicap? During the second semester of my freshman year at the University of Arizona I encountered this issue in one of my classes.

To solve this problem, I had to talk to my academic adviser about the issues that I was facing in a course. He could give me the necessary forms to fill out to withdraw myself from the course. In addition, I had to write a formal letter to the dean of the university regarding the instructor's refusal to accommodate me as a person with a disability. As a result, I received a "W" on my transcript. This meant that the dean could approve my request to leave a class past the drop deadline. This taught me that many people are not willing to change their teaching styles, workplaces, or other tasks to treat a person with a disability equally.

Helping Others Learn

I believe that many of my teachers had questions about having a blind student in their classes. Many of them were unsure about how I would do basic assignments such as completing science labs, drawing, writing compositions, or researching different topics online. I made it my duty to ease the anxieties of my instructors as I spent time after or during class to communicate with my instructors and receive their feedback. For example, in my linguistics class, one of the requirements was to draw tree diagrams for different languages that included the syntax of the language. On the first day of the syntax course, I met with my instructor to discuss having a note taker draw the tree diagrams on a paper that would raise the drawings into a tactile format. In addition, my instructor and I worked during his office hours on these diagrams if my note taker was not available. This is just one of the many instances when my instructors had questions about how to accommodate a totally blind student. My willingness to learn allowed many of them to realize that a person does not need to be treated unfairly based on their limitations.

LIFE AFTER COLLEGE

Moving Forward to Inspire

Since my graduation from the University of Arizona, I have experienced success upon returning to Southern California to acquire work experience. I have involved myself in temporary paid positions at organizations such as the Braille Institute of America, Junior Blind of America, and Blind Children's Learning Center. At these organizations, I have taught children, youth, and adults the importance of Braille literacy and competency and how to live life as a sightless individual with a positive attitude. These organizations have a common goal: independence. Independence is one of the essential values for a person with a disability, especially in the blind community. It is important for people without sight to realize that they can perform daily tasks at a job, in the community, or in the educational system if provided with the right support. I strongly believe that there is still work that needs to be done regarding accommodations for people with disabilities. Every day, many schools and workplaces are learning how to appropriately accommodate individuals who are physically or mentally challenged.

MY RECOMMENDATIONS FOR WORKING WITH THE BLIND

How can persons with disabilities educate others about treatment in and out of the classroom? There are a few answers to this question. To begin, it is important for individuals with a disability to know what accommodations they need. It is the responsibility of students and individuals to know how and why certain accommodations should be made in the community, workplace, and classroom. This allows people to understand how accommodations create a positive change and learning environment for everyone. Not only must the disabled community know their accommodations, but they must also take advantage of teachable moments.

Unfortunately, society is often not willing to accept people who have a handicap. Thus teachable moments allow individuals without disabilities to learn how to be empathetic. Throughout my 16 years of education, I experienced many teachable moments with my sighted peers and instructors. Everyone could learn about how a blind person describes pictures, plays sports, and even creates artwork. Teachable moments should not just remain in a classroom, as every day provides moments to teach people how to develop a positive environment about an individual who has a disability.

Even though teachable moments are necessary, not everyone is willing to receive them. There are consequences for not respecting the needs of a person with a disability. Discrimination toward the disabled community violates laws in the Americans with Disabilities Act. For instance, it is illegal for drivers to refuse service to individuals with service animals. These violations can lead to lawsuits, protests toward a certain company or agency, or even meetings with Congress about discriminatory acts. It is important to continue to remind educators, companies, and the community that it can be done. Just because someone has physical or mental limitations doesn't mean that he or she should be discriminated against due to their condition. Keep in mind, discrimination toward people with disabilities will continue to happen. It is up to us to push past the pain and wounds of unfavorable treatment and move forward with confidence. Change does not happen overnight, as it can take months and years to make a difference. However, nothing is impossible to accomplish as my narrative describes: It can be done!

REFERENCES

ADA Central. (2016). *ADA compliance info.* Retrieved May 19, 2017, from http://adacentral.com/compliance/

Blind Children's Learning Center. (2016). *Our mission.* Retrieved May 19, 2017, from www.blindkids.org/our-mission.html

DelPo, A. (2017). *Reasonable accommodations for people with disabilities: The ADA.* Retrieved from www.nolo.com/.../reasonable-accommodations-people-with-disabilities -29492

Garwa, D. (2015, July 28). *Why do we want to send our special needs children to mainstream schools?* Retrieved May 19, 2017, from http://www.twominuteparenting.com/

Giasone, B. (2009, June 17). Blind girl meets the challenges to graduate high school. *Orange County Register.* Retrieved from https://www.ocregister.com/2009/06/17/blind-girl-meets-the-challenges-to-graduate-high-school/

National Eye Institute. (2014, June). *Facts about retinopathy of prematurity.* Retrieved May 19, 2017 from https://nei.nih.gov/health/rop/rop

STEP community workshops. (n.d.). Retrieved from www.wayfinderfamily.org/program/youth-transition-services

CHAPTER 7

OTOSCLEROSIS

The Invisible Disease

Aunye Boone
Self-Employed Actor and English Educator

ABSTRACT

What would the world be like without the ability to hear? A dark and mysterious place. In this chapter, writer Aunye Boone takes the reader through a journey of hope, pride, and self-advocacy. Things aren't always as they seem, and looking at Aunye from the outside, you would think she is a well-put-together former Virginia Tech athlete and academic. Inside, her hearing is failing her slowly, and without a frightening incident that occurred, she would not have realized the severity of her disability. The stigma of having hearing loss is sometimes associated with people thinking you could be mentally challenged or that you cannot fend for yourself. This chapter debunks the most common myths that hearing loss is a disease that consumes your life. Hearing loss does not become a person's identity; you have the power to take your disability and define it yourself.

Untold Narratives, pages 97–103
Copyright © 2018 by Information Age Publishing

ALTERNATE REALITY

Denial is such a deep-rooted seed that lays between hope, despair, and the truth. I was raised knowing that I had to excel in my studies, respect my elders, and stay healthy. Hearing loss and deafness were not subjects that my peers or elders spoke about. So as my hearing began to fade as a teenager, I did not know how to express this issue. My hearing loss became a special secret that only belonged to me. What was wrong with a simple "Huh?" in a large, noisy crowd? I figured this made me unique and curious. Growing up in southern Maryland, I always felt as if I had a fun and positive childhood without any major conflicts.

As a child, I was always curious about the world around me and why things happened the way they did. I was, and always will be, on the hunt for answers, happy endings, and reassurance that fate did her job in the end. Balancing my first love of acting and the gift of running that God gave me, I always knew that life would go smoothly and I had options if there was any hurdle in my way. While attending Calvert High School, I was a three-time Classical Monologue Winner for the state of Maryland and a nine-time individual state champion for Maryland track and field.

Between sore hips from dancing in my school musicals, pulled hamstrings from improper warmups at the track, and two broken toes, I had had my fair share of common bumps and bruises that teenagers receive. I took all honors and advanced placement courses in high school, and graduated with a 3.8 GPA. The Calvert County Public School system created an environment that was nurturing, interactive, and accommodating to everyone's learning styles. I liked to take an assignment and make it my own, and with many of my school projects and papers, I flourished in such a creative environment.

Waiting behind the protective and nurturing doors of my high school was the real world, for which I was not necessarily prepared. As an African-American woman at my high school, I was placed on a high pedestal due to breaking many stereotypical barriers in the classroom and on the track. The reality is that college and the real world both have many African-American women who are blazing their own career paths and setting high goals just like me.

Just like the big fish in the small pond, I felt secure in my hometown. I did not enter college equipped with the resources for staying on top of my health beyond the usual doctor and dentist visits. The high schools in Calvert County are required to give concussion tests and sports physicals; never any hearing tests or school eye exams. Passing the physical and concussion tests at my school each year, I was under the impression that I was healthy and normal just like everyone else. Everyone blasts music in their cars? Other people sometimes struggle to hear conversations and television, right?

Freshman Blues

I entered my freshman year of college at Virginia Tech on a full athletic scholarship, and was accepted into the honors Political Science Department. The first semester of college proved to be an upward battle; I had a poor handle on my schedule and time management, and my GPA suffered. Each weekday I had 6 a.m. runs with the track team, a full schedule of college courses, 2 p.m. track workouts, 4 p.m. weightlifting, and 8 p.m. mandatory study hall. Although my day was blocked out strictly for me, I quickly lost the focus of my mission at Virginia Tech: to successfully graduate and leave a lasting impact. Thus, the fall 2008 semester for me meant waking up and walking through my day as I was told, but feeling no motivation or control over my own education. I was merely a ghost of myself that semester, floating around doing what I was told to do, but not having the crutch of my creative former high school network to help me along the way. With rigorous schedules come very serious expectations, and I could not handle the workload and properly study.

Due to the large class sizes at Virginia Tech, I found myself immersed in a sea of lost individuals like myself who rarely took notes, could not hear the professors, and simply just "existed" in class with no active participation. Returning home for Christmas break, I received a notification from my track coach that I was on academic probation, removed from the Honors Political Science Program, and would be suspended from Virginia Tech if I had another failing semester. The 3.8 GPA perfectionist from high school slipped to a 1.75 GPA in college, and I was in denial about how this even happened. Calvert High School did not prepare me for this moment; this moment where my grades would essentially define me. I was simply a number at Virginia Tech, a seat in my professors' classes, and a workhorse on the track to provide the track team with winning points. I no longer felt like the prize possession of Calvert High School anymore; my glory days there had come and gone.

LASTING HOKIE FOOTPRINTS

With motivation and encouragement from my mother to pursue what truly made me happy and inspired me, I returned to Virginia Tech for spring semester and walked into the English Department to change my major. From the moment I walked in, the air about this place felt inspiring and creative; just what I was missing in my education. The professors in this major allowed the students to take ownership of their work under set guidelines, and we had smaller classrooms where each student felt like they were contributing to the conversation.

I felt like my voice was finally beginning to be heard, and I could also hear what others were truly saying. From spring semester until graduation in 2008, I made the dean's list each time, ultimately graduating cum laude from Virginia Tech. Throughout those 4 years at Virginia Tech, I became the ACC Rookie of the Year, was nominated for Virginia Tech Woman of the Year, was the student star at the VT Billion Dollar Campaign Event, and traveled to Vietnam to coach and teach underprivileged children. After finding community and a major to be passionate about, the seed inside of me continued to grow and make lasting impressions upon the Hokie campus. I consider these impressions to be that of the Hokie mascot: unique, large, and encompassing a range of talents and growth through adversity.

OTOSCLEROSIS: THE INVISIBLE DISABILITY

This story was supposed to be about denial, right? While you may think this is the beginning of a healthy, vivacious young lady who is about to begin her young adult life in the working world, this story quickly turns. Otosclerosis is a silent, invisible disease that is a rare genetic disorder that causes hearing loss due to the ear's inability to generate sound. What does that have to do with me? How could this affect a woman in her 20s who up until now seemingly made it without knowing she had a disability? This disease is rare in African Americans, and mostly affects middle-aged Caucasian women. I was the rare African-American woman, in my 20s, who was officially diagnosed with otosclerosis in September of 2015.

The symptoms and warning signs were there, but I refused to acknowledge that anything was wrong. The summer prior to my diagnosis, I began having major issues with my balance and blockage in my ears; I assumed it was just my severe allergies kicking in. As my ears buzzed loudly one night while i was in bed, I started remembering my college days: my struggle to hear sound on the television, the muffled sounds of the coaches' instructions at large track meets where the voices blended together, as well as my signature loud car volume. My mother and brother always made comments about the volume of my television whenever I was home, and I would respond with "I watch my TV like it's a movie theater experience; I just prefer for it to be loud."

I became the master of lip reading and trying to decipher what people were saying in groups because I only heard whispers. Back to the summer of 2015, I finished grocery shopping with my mother and began taking the shopping cart back to the store as she was unloading groceries. As I approached the store, I noticed that my mother and brother were running to me and flagging me down; they had been screaming my name and warning me that a car was about to hit me. I had no clue that a car was behind me, and in that moment I knew that my hearing was affecting my safety. Had

I been alone or had the driver inside of the car kept driving, I could have been seriously injured. My thoughts began racing to my fear of not being able to hear a person's footsteps if they were approaching to kidnap me or cause harm. I knew this was serious and I had to seek medical attention.

Expert Opinion

I went to my local ENT specialist in Calvert County, still hanging on to the false hope that this was a severe blockage in my ears from allergies. The specialist did an ear, nose, and throat check and explained that she could find nothing wrong. The specialist then sent me to the audiologist in the same office who conducted a hearing test. My last hearing test was in elementary school. I never had it checked in middle school, high school, or even in my sports physicals in college. I went into the hearing test and soon realized I could not hear the directions that were being given to me. In one test I had to repeat the sounds and words that the operator gave me; and as the decibels of sound began to diminish, so did my hearing.

Struggling to hear small bell tones and beeps became the next obstacle, and I was sweating by the end of the test from humiliation and shock. How could a person so seemingly put together be unable to hear how normal people hear? I felt confused, lost, and it took me back to feeling like I was in a public place again surrounded by tons of people yet feeling like they were whispering. The results of the exam were that I had severe hearing loss similar to an elderly person who is hard of hearing. The specialists in Calvert County could not treat me; I was referred to a surgeon named Dr. Eisenman who specialized in hearing located at the University of Maryland Baltimore Medical Center.

At my first appointment with Dr. Eisenman, he conducted his own set of hearing tests, and within an hour told me that I indeed had otosclerosis. With a combination of the ENT and the diagnosis at the University of Maryland, Baltimore, it was recommended that I get surgery within two weeks or take the second option of having hearing aids for the rest of my life. Hearing aids would end up being a yearly investment going into the thousands, but I had fears of a life-changing surgery. Candidly, Dr. Eisenman said "Aunye, if you don't take the option of surgery, just be aware that you are progressively going deaf, and at the rate that you are losing your hearing, you could be deaf before middle age."

Due to having a lead role in a professional theater production with the Compass Rose Theatre, I pushed the surgery out for four weeks so that I could finish the show. When I told my cast mates that I had hearing loss, they had no clue about my struggle because I picked up on stage directions, owned the stage, and never missed a beat during rehearsals when we ran lines. Due to the severity and risks of the surgery, Dr. Eisenman chose to only perform surgery on my left ear, and then to follow-up with surgery on the right ear a year or two later.

After finishing my show, I had surgery in October and was full of apprehension and fear beforehand. On the day of the surgery, I still had various questions for myself: Why did I decide to go through with this surgery; what if the surgery doesn't work out and I leave the hospital worse than when I entered? Waking up from my ethereal slumber, I realized that I indeed had a very successful surgery and was surrounded by my mother and aunt, support on social media, and the warm and comforting hospital staff. During my first trip to use the bathroom, I had to be assisted by a nurse because the surgery affected my balance for a few days.

I wobbled and leaned upon the nurse and could hear my ears ringing as sounds began coming to life. Leaving the hospital in a wheelchair, I was given instructions to lay in bed and refrain from driving for a week, and from flying for a month. For the first few weeks after my surgery, I would rest my head at night and hear what sounded like waves of the ocean. This was due to the blood and packing inside my ear after the surgeon cut through my ear drum and shaved my middle ear bone to put the implant in. For a month, my meals tasted like metal due to my temporal nerve being moved during the surgery.

ADVOCATING FOR THOSE WITH NO VOICE

My downtime and recovery taught me patience, self-care, and allowed me to research and find what information I could find about other people who had dealt with this disease. Oddly enough, I found limited information on otosclerosis and many of the videos available on YouTube were from medical professionals. I wanted to hear real life stories and to connect with people who could empathize with me. Taking the initiative, I created my own community and otosclerosis network. I began by posting authentic photos before and after the surgery on Facebook and Instagram, and I uploaded a YouTube video that chronicled my journey to discovering and dealing with otosclerosis.

Within weeks, I started receiving messages from people as far away as Spain and France who had otosclerosis and were inspired by my story. Many of the people who had this disease expressed their fears and anxiety going into the story. Their nerves were calmed when they watched my video and found that I had success from this surgery. My YouTube video now has roughly 2,500 views, and I hope that people around the world continue to share their experiences with this rare, genetic disease, which comes so silently but so rapidly. I am proud of taking ownership and pride in my disability, and have used my voice to advocate for myself and for others.

In the fall of 2016, I joined the Hearing Loss Association of America as an advocate, and participated in the DC Walk4Hearing, where people of all ages, genders, and races came together to raise awareness and money to further research on hearing loss and provide innovative solutions for hearing. Although I now have 100% hearing in my left ear, I still have to get surgery in my right ear performed soon. I pray that my second surgery goes smoothly, and that I will be able to join the rest of the world in hearing sounds in their entirety again. For now, I hold my head high, and walk proudly with my titanium implant fit so securely in my ear.

Hearing is crucial, and is not something that should be taken for granted. The basics that most humans have are sight, sound, taste, and touch. My ability to hear sound was almost taken from me, and without taking the necessary action to advocate for myself and create my own network of support and allies, I would not be where I am today. For the person reading my chapter right now, I implore you to go with a family member and get an annual hearing exam; even if you feel like you can hear well, still take preventative measures and see how your hearing compares with the stats of everyone else in America.

In the future, I'll know that if I have kids, they will need to get annual exams because I am a carrier of this disease. As of now, I live in the moment and when I wake up and can hear the sound of the trash men coming to pick up the trash in my driveway, I know that my day will be off to a good start. God's provisions and mercy on my life have been wonderful; what people may see as a disability, has become my greatest strength and a platform to share with the world. No amount of riches, academic achievements, or professional success could give me the story that I have now.

CHAPTER 8

NOT ABOUT THE DISABILITY, BUT THE ABILITY TO SUCCEED

Oluwakemi Elufiede
Carnegie Writers, Inc.

ABSTRACT

African-American students have faced numerous obstacles within the academic system, especially in special education. Many students have encountered teachers who frame their learning from a deficit perspective. And since 1973, the epidemic of special education services has impacted teaching, learning, rehabilitation, and employment. However, as a subgroup African Americans with disabilities still lag behind their counterparts, and the stories of women with disabilities are untold. Therefore, to assist students academically, classroom strategies should focus on the individuals receiving services and not the individuals providing the services. Thus, this chapter strives to employ a personal perspective based on a lived experience, lessons learned, mentoring, advocacy, and accessibility to resources. Moreover, the chapter covers six emerging themes from my own experiences that are: (a) the label, (b) my understanding, (c) the transition, (d) reevaluation, (e) the aftermath, and (f) recovery.

Untold Narratives, pages 105–112
Copyright © 2018 by Information Age Publishing
All rights of reproduction in any form reserved.

PERSONAL NARRATIVE: MY JOURNEY

The Label

The recognition of my disability was discovered in elementary school. In the second grade, my teacher noticed that I was falling behind and recommended educational and psychological testing. I was diagnosed with attention-deficit/hyperactivity disorder (ADHD) and a specific learning disability, which arises "from neurological differences in brain structure and function and affect a person's ability to receive, store, process, retrieve or communicate information" (Cortiella & Horowitz, 2014). Attention-deficit/hyperactivity disorder has become more widely known and children are usually overdiagnosed (Morin, 2017).

Although, at the time I never really understood what ADHD meant, I do recall having difficulty concentrating in class and on daily activities. I never considered myself "disabled," but based on teacher recommendations, I needed academic support. I remember participating in several individual education plan (IEP) meetings and feeling discouraged because some teachers framed my learning from a "deficit" perspective while others took interest in my "abilities," which motivated me.

According to my psychological evaluations over the years, my IQ was below 70, which meant that a person was intellectually disabled (once referred to as mental retardation). According to the American Association on Intellectual and Developmental Disabilities (2017):

> Mental retardation is a lifelong condition of impaired or incomplete mental development. According to the most widely used definition of mental retardation, it is characterized by three criteria: significantly sub average intellectual functioning; concurrent and related limitations in two or more adaptive skill areas; and manifestation before age eighteen. The first step for diagnosing and classifying a person as having mental retardation is for a qualified person to give one or more standardized intelligence tests and a standardized adaptive skills test on an individual basis.

According to the American Psychological Association (2017), such psychological evaluations serve as an assessment tool to measure and observe behavior, and to diagnosis and guide interventions for individuals experiencing difficulties in schools. After many years, I began to understand why I was provided with additional academic assistance. Compared to my grade level, I lacked intellectual skills to comprehend content; however, I was always told by my teachers and psychologists that the test did not influence my academic performance and progression to the next grade level. This was false, as it impacted my ability to enhance the required skills for advancement.

My Understanding

In middle school, my teachers began to set me apart because I was in special education classes for English and math. I remember feeling isolated from peers and wondering if there would be any chance of succeeding. With support from family and teachers, I participated in a mainstream classroom setting where I could recognize my academic abilities. I was different from my school peers because I did not feel as smart as they were, which became a challenge. I felt alone and had anxiety about my inability to keep up, but I could retain academic content with appropriate support. Even with these challenges, I figured out that by receiving academic and social support and getting advice from others, I would succeed with a lot of effort. The transition was hard, but by the time I got to high school, my education started to thrive.

Before high school, I moved to a new school district in another state, which provided me with services comparable to those in the original IEP (Wright, 2016). The move was a challenge and an interesting experience as I had to complete another evaluation with the school psychologist. The findings revealed that I did not have a learning disability. Rather, I was diagnosed with a mental illness, defined by the American Psychiatric Association (2015) as "health conditions involving changes in thinking, emotion or behavior (or a combination of these) . . . associated with distress and/or problems functioning in social, work or family activities."

The new school district was not that advanced, and the curriculum was not consistent with the regular education curriculum for special education students. I was placed in special education classes for English and reading—which reminded me of first grade—where I would write sentences with spelling words and complete spelling tests, which were not consistent with my academic abilities. This caused increased anxiety, particularly in academic situations because I was not being challenged academically with the assignments for my grade level.

I was aware of my abilities, but felt different from my peers because of feedback from my teachers. There were teachers that noticed my academic strengths and wanted to engage me further, so they guided me through additional grade level material for practice. They pushed me to go the extra mile and recommended that I make a transition from special education classes. These teachers and school representatives worked together to develop the appropriate *accommodations* to "meet the individual student needs and ensure equal access to the academic content standards" (Beech, 2010, p. 4). These accommodations allowed me to have better access to the curriculum and to improve my academic self-esteem.

The Transition

The difference between middle school and high school was that the special education curriculum was not on the same grade level. According to National Center on Secondary Education and Training (2017) the Individuals with Disabilities Education Act of 1997 stated that curriculum must be aligned with the educational standards. These limitations impact academic growth because they do not allow students to perform at their full potential. After a while, I got closer to graduation and prepared for the graduation examination. I did not pass the science and social studies section after several attempts, and received a Special Education diploma, which did not allow my advancement into postsecondary educational institutions. Those who are looking to graduate know about the graduation requirements that need to be fulfilled. This is also understood by their families, who help them develop a 4-year plan to earn a diploma that will not only recognize the graduate's accomplishments, but also will envision the future. This provides opportunities with potential employers and for postsecondary and continuing education.

After high school, I studied to earn my GED since I was not motivated and confident in taking the graduation exam again after several failures. I had anxiety about the process, but overcame my fear to pursue the goal of getting into a college. During this journey, I was informed about a private school that could provide a regular education diploma. Even with my anxiety, I tried to become successful in achieving my goals. Through the academic support at the private school, I received my regular education diploma. Without the opportunity to transfer, I would not have been able to start college immediately after high school. Because of this experience, I decided to major in special education to provide support to students, make a difference, and change the direction of special education services in the public-school sector.

Reevaluate

Attending college had its own challenges as I took the math and English placement exams to determine whether I was required to take remedial classes. I also met with the disability office to apply for accommodations. I was informed that I had to be reevaluated before being eligible to receive services at the college level. I was diagnosed with dysthymic disorder, a mild form of depression (Morrison, 2016). With this diagnosis, it was recommended that I receive accommodations that assisted me using techniques for study skills and test-taking strategies to eliminate my anxiety

With support, I could excel academically and socially, and establish clear career goals. Vocational rehabilitation programs, "state run, federally funded programs that offer a way for people with mental and physical disabilities to get the help they need to become more independent and to go back to work," assisted in paying for my college education, career advisement, and job placement (Linebaugh, 2017). During college, I refined my skills for careers in social services, higher education, public education, and the nonprofit sector. This experience impacted my career choices with employment, community, and volunteer opportunities.

The Aftermath

I am now an educator, author, editor, poet, and entrepreneur with more than 10 years of professional experience in public, higher, and community education, in addition to my endeavors in the nonprofit sector and social services. As the founder and president of Carnegie Writers, Inc., and K&E Educational Consulting Services, I provide assistance with writing, editing, nonprofit management, life coaching, and publishing. Prior to entrepreneurship, I assumed many roles as a tutor, teacher, mentor, instructor, evaluations manager, case manager, and residence director. In these various roles, I implemented and facilitated programs for the improvement of literacy and writing skills; behavioral health and developmental disabilities; career and workforce development; and personal growth and development.

I am the founder of three community-based adult writing groups in Savannah, Georgia; Huntsville, Alabama; and Nashville, Tennessee. I have presented at more than 20 professional conferences and workshops; and facilitated more than 30 programs in residence life, leadership development, writing, literacy, technology, career and workforce development, effective tutoring strategies, mental health, self-directed learning, community education, adult learning, and mentoring. I have developed course and training materials for creative writing workshops, freshmen orientations, information literacy, teen/adult author workshops, and literacy achievement programs.

I am also a member of the American Association of Adult and Continuing Education (AAACE), the Association for the Study of Higher Education (ASHE), the American Association of University Women (AAUW), the American Educational Research Association (AERA), and Carnegie Writers (CW). In 2015, I served as the director on the Adult Higher Education Alliance (AHEA) board of directors and the chief editor for conference proceedings. I also served as the newsletter editor for AAACE and the lead editor for the CW book series. I am the editor and author of six books and have several academic publications. Because of my continuous engagement, I was recognized as Outstanding Leader for Girl Scouts of Historic Georgia, nominated for the Phenomenal Women Award by the Scarritt Bennett Center, and the national Big Brother and Big Sister volunteer of the year award.

Recovery

Through these experiences, I have been able to give back to local communities through advocacy, teaching, and outreach. My lived experiences and personal drive have allowed me to overcome setbacks and challenges through my education and cope with my disability, which has been a healing process. With recovery and experience, I have learned how to advocate for myself and others. These skills encouraged me to access resources based on individualized needs. Because of external challenges and societal expectations, I learned to think more creatively about effective problem-solving techniques and person-centered planning, which involves developing skills, building relationships, and working in teams. This is an integral part of an individual's life because it promotes self-reflection, support from others, and long-term and short-term goals.

RECOMMENDATIONS

Educators, administrators, and community members are the key stakeholders that can stimulate change for people with disabilities. They must change their approach by eliminating stereotypical assumptions and opinions, by looking at every individual with an open mind. For consistent support, there must be rapport building, recognition of strengths, resourcefulness, and flexibility. Relationship building is crucial for reaching anyone, especially individuals with disabilities. It is integral that a rapport is developed through a gradual process that is not forced or demanding. People want to be valued for their experiences and respected for their differences as this builds trust. With a strong relationship, individual strengths will prevail and encourage further suggestions for success in daily activities and educational pursuits. People need consistent support as their disability will sometimes impact their ability to recognize their strengths, which will aid in coping with their challenges.

Resourcefulness is the key to advancement for personal growth and development, as well as the key to locating available resources to help people with (and without) disabilities with outcomes, objectives, and experiments, as well as negotiate challenges (Price-Mitchell, 2015). There are always new resources being developed to support diversity and individuality. For people with disabilities, this enables rehabilitation toward continuing education, employment, and career opportunities, as well as assistance with health care and mental health.

Stakeholders must understand that there are individual limitations, so they are better able to provide the best resources for long-lasting results. Furthermore, providing support can be difficult, but flexibility is the key to meeting the needs of people with disabilities. Throughout my academic career from primary school to college, those who supported me were there to encourage me through difficult times. When attending groups or meetings, I realized that there were others like me. This allowed me to reflect on what needed to be done, to take responsibility, and to find ways to create solutions and challenge myself. It helped me build my character, and provide aspiration to support others.

CONCLUSION

With my deep faith in God and the support of family and friends, I have gained more confidence and self-motivation. I have realized that resources for people with disabilities are important for their transition from childhood to adulthood within the education system. Social services and school districts need to reevaluate how they deal with individual students by finding ways to encourage strategic person-centered planning. My experiences prepared me for success, and despite challenges the future should be based on lessons learned.

Remaining in the past does not promote progressive change for people with disabilities. There should be positive results and goals that are incorporated with supportive measures within the community, schools, and social services. To do this, there must be a continuous evaluation of what works and what does not. The transition from primary to adult education has brought me to where I can help those in the community who are dealing with the same setbacks. My approach focuses on strengthening skills to eliminate weaknesses. With better community outreach, more lives can be impacted through the support of mentors and individuals facing the same challenges.

REFERENCES

American Association on Intellectual and Developmental Disabilities. (2017). *Mental retardation: An overview.* Retrieved from https://www.hrw.org/reports/2001/ustat/ustat0301-01.htm#P214_26786

American Psychiatric Association. (2015, November). *What is mental illness?* Retrieved June 21, 2017, from https://www.psychiatry.org/patients-families/what-is-mental-illness

American Psychological Association. (2017). *Understanding psychological testing and assessment.* Retrieved June 21, 2017, from http://www.apa.org/helpcenter/assessment.aspx

Beech, M. (2010). *Accommodations: Assisting students with disabilities* (3rd ed.). Retrieved from http://www.fldoe.org/core/fileparse.php/7690/urlt/0070069-accomm-educator.pdf

Cortiella, C., & Horowitz, S. (2014). *The state of learning disabilities: Facts and emerging issues* (3rd ed.). Retrieved from https://www.ncld.org/wp-content/uploads/2014/11/2014-State-of-LD.pdf

Linebaugh, M. (2017). *Vocational rehabilitation for individuals with disabilities.* Retrieved from https://www.nolo.com/legal-encyclopedia/vocational-rehabilitation-individuals-with-disabilities.html

Morin, A. (2017). *A timeline of learning and attention issues.* Retrieved June 21, 2017, from https://www.understood.org/en/learning-attention-issues/getting-started/what-you-need-to-know/a-timeline-of-learning-and-attention-issues

Morrison, J. R. (2006). *DSM-IV made easy: The clinician's guide to diagnosis* (Rev. ed.). New York, NY: Guilford Press.

Price-Mitchell, M. (2015, July 13). *Teaching for life success: Why resourcefulness matters* (Blog post). Retrieved from https://www.edutopia.org/blog/8-pathways-why-resourcefulness-matters-marilyn-price-mitchell

The National Center on Secondary Education and Transition (2017). *Key provisions on Transition IDEA 1997 compared to H.R. 1350 IDEA 2004.* Retrieved from http://www.ncset.org/publications/related/ideatransition.pdf

Wright, P. (2016, October 12). *Changing schools and IEPs.* Retrieved June 21, 2017, from https://www.hrw.org/reports/2001/ustat/ustat0301-01.htm#P214_26786

PART IV

CULTURAL CAPITAL CLASSROOM ACTIVITY

CULTURAL CAPITAL CLASSROOM ACTIVITY

A pedagogical practice that may improve students' knowledge is critical literacy (CL), which is based on a sociocultural philosophy of language that focuses on teaching students to discern the connection between language and power (Shor & Freire, 2003). Particularly, while some Eurocentric instruction and curriculum leaves students feeling uncomfortable because the texts do not relate to them, such instruction (CL) may help AA students with disabilities co-construct deeper meaning about power and inequality (McDonald, Keys, & Balcazar, 2007; Murray & Naranjo, 2008). For this population to become engaged, preK–12 teachers may want to consider employing a variety of pedagogical practices (cultural capital activities; Ford, 2013). Sociologist Pierre Bourdieu (1986) defines cultural capital as knowledge, disposition, and skills that are passed down from one generation to another.

Teachers combining students' cultural perspectives and lived experiences with classroom content may enhance students' beliefs, attitudes, values, and the capital they bring to the classroom as well as their academic engagement (Gillborn, 2015; Orellana, Reynolds, & Martinez, 2011). Employing sociocultural perspectives and cultural capital activities can allow students to bring their knowledge and understanding of the world to the classroom (Gavelek & Bresnahan, 2009; Sweet & Snow, 2003).

Thereafter, once AA students with disabilities access the discourse and receive effective literacy instruction, they can serve as voices for other

Untold Narratives, pages 115–120
Copyright © 2018 by Information Age Publishing
All rights of reproduction in any form reserved.

students and become valued, contributing members of society (Moje, Luke, Davies, & Street, 2009). Furthermore, after reading these narratives, teachers may consider requiring students to interrogate their own positionality within the special education system by drafting their own narratives and reflecting on their lived experiences by choosing from the following social assets (Robinson, 2017). The objective is to be as creative as possible (see Appendix A for structuring a personal narrative).

A NARRATIVE ABOUT ASPIRATIONAL CAPITAL

This type of capital emphasizes the ability to maintain hope and a vision for a brighter future despite what may be impossible odds otherwise (Yosso, 2005, p. 77). Questions to reflect on:

- How and why you have overcome adversity in your life
- How you made a way out of your situation
- What you did to get here today and why

A NARRATIVE ABOUT LINGUISTIC CAPITAL

This type of capital emphasizes the cognitive abilities and social skills that students use to maneuver through their "space" by utilizing one or more languages and speaking styles (Yosso, 2005, p. 79; see Appendix B for resources about different kinds of English). Questions to reflect on:

- What did you do and why?
- What do you think of this today?
- How do you think that impacted you? Or, what do you do, linguistically, in different situations and why?

A NARRATIVE ABOUT FAMILIAL CAPITAL

This type of capital is about the systems of knowledge that family members have instilled in the memories and cultural values of the students. The idea is that the stories, warnings, expectations, or legacies handed down through families shape identities and reactions to situations outside of the home. Topics can include a family story, tradition, saying, or belief system that is part of a student's ethnicity, which can be similar to or different from other family capital or values (Yosso, 2005, p. 79). Questions to reflect on:

- How has this influenced you?
- Did this ever cause conflict with peers, teachers, administrators, or institutions? If so, what did you do about it?
- How do you think this has impacted you?

A NARRATIVE ABOUT SOCIAL CAPITAL

This type of capital is about community resources (church, after-school programs, organizations, or peer groups) that have helped students become who they are. The students should describe how an affiliation has played an important role in their lives by taking readers inside to see, feel, and hear who the students were as members of these affiliations (Yosso, 2005, p. 79). The students should focus on how these connections have impacted them.

A NARRATIVE ABOUT NAVIGATIONAL CAPITAL AND RESISTANT CAPITAL

These types of capital help one to confront oppression and provide unique social skills, resilience, and cultural values. Students should focus on the events that have taught them how to resist oppression and/or the status quo (Yosso, 2005, p. 80). Questions to reflect on:

- How does this impact you?
- Why are you connected to this?
- How do you think these connections have impacted you?

As the guest editor, I am pleased to share this set of readings with the hope that they improve the academic outcomes of AA students in and out of special education. This group has been neglected for far too long, which has resulted in numerous and extensive gaps in knowledge, theory, and academic support (Robinson, 2016). I am aware that this collection neither fills all voids nor meets all needs. Nonetheless, it offers much in the fields of multicultural education, special education, and beyond.

APPENDIX A
Structure of a Personal Narrative Essay

https://www.sbcc.edu/clrc/files/wl/downloads/StructureofaPersonal
NarrativeEssay.pdf

Introduction

Begin your paper with a "hook" that catches the reader's attention and sets the scene. Where is the event set? What time of year? How old were you when this happened? State your thesis: what you learned, or how the event is significant to you.

Body Paragraph

Show, Don't Tell

Good storytelling includes details and descriptions that help the reader understand what the writer has experienced. Think about using all five senses—not just the sense of sight—to add details about what you heard, saw, and felt during the event.

Supporting Evidence

Your experience acts as the evidence that proves your thesis. The events of the story should demonstrate the lesson learned, or the significance of the event to you.

Passage of Time

Writing about the events of your experience using time chronologically, from beginning to end, is the most common and clearest way to tell a story. Whether you choose to write chronologically or not, use transition words to clearly indicate to the reader what happened first, next, and last.

Transitions

In a narrative essay, a new paragraph marks a change in the action of a story, or a move from action to reflection. Paragraphs should connect to one another

Conclusion

Analyze and reflect on the action of the story, including how events are significant to you.

APPENDIX B
Resources on Linguistic Capital
(Different Kinds of English)

- Amy Tan's essay "Mother Tongue"
  http://www.essayjudge.com/document_detail.php?doc_id=219
- Gloria Anzaldua's essay "How to Tame a Wild Tongue"
  https://singleadelman.pbworks.com/w/file/fetch/66649007/
  Language-Composition-FWHS-Essay-5.pdf
- Vershawn Ashanti Young "Your Average Nigga Performing Race,
  Literacy, and Masculinity"
  http://www.wsupress.wayne.edu/books/detail/your-average-nigga

REFERENCES

Bourdieu, P. (1986). The forms of capital. In J. Richardson (Ed.) *Handbook of theory and research for the sociology of education* (pp. 241–258). New York, NY: Greenwood Press.

Ford, D. Y. (2013). *Recruiting and retaining culturally different students in gifted education.* Waco, TX: Prufrock Press.

Gavelek, J., & Bresnahan, P. (2009). Ways of meaning making: Sociocultural perspective reading comprehension. In S. E. Israel, & G. G. Duffy (Eds.), *Handbook of research on reading comprehension* (pp. 289–306). New York, NY: Routledge.

Gillborn, D. (2015). Intersectionality, critical race theory, and the primacy of racism: Race, class, gender, and disability in education. *Qualitative Inquiry, 21*(3), 277–287.

McDonald, K. E., Keys, C. B., & Balcazar, F. B. (2007). Disability, race/ethnicity and gender: Themes of cultural oppression, acts of individual resistance. *American Journal of Community Psychology, 39,* 145–161.

Moje, E. B., Luke, A., Davis, B., & Street, B. (2009). Literacy and identity: Examining the metaphors in history and contemporary research. *Reading Research Quarterly, 44*(4), 415–437.

Murray, C., & Naranjo, J. (2008). Poor, Black, learning disabled, and graduating: An investigation of factors and processes associated with school completion among high-risk urban youth. *Remedial and Special Education, 29*(3), 145–160.

Orellana, M. F., Reynolds, J., & Martinez, D. C. (2011). Cultural modeling: Building on cultural strengths as an alternative to remedial reading approaches. In A. McGill-Franzen & R. L. Allington (Eds.), *Handbook of reading disability research* (pp. 273–278). New York, NY: Routledge.

Robinson, S. A. (2016). Can't c me. *Review of Disability Studies, 12*(4), 1–4.

Robinson, S. A. (2017). "Me against the world": Autoethnographic poetry. *Disability & Society, 32*(5), 748–752.

Shor, I., & Freire, P. (2003). What are the fears and risks of transformation. In A. Darder, M. P. Baltodano, & R. Torres (Eds.), *The critical pedagogy reader* (pp. 479–497). New York, NY: Routledge.

Sweet, A. P., & Snow, C., E. (2003). *Rethinking reading comprehension.* New York, NY: Guilford.

Yosso, T. J. (2005). Whose culture has capital? A critical race theory discussion of community cultural wealth. *Race, Ethnicity and Education, 8*(1), 69–91.

AFTERWORD

Nina F. Weisling

"But these kids can't do grade level math!"

The teacher speaking was an early-20s White woman not long out of college, placed in a "high needs" special education classroom through an alternative certification program. I was a few years younger than her, in my first months of full-time mentoring, fresh out of a middle school special education classroom on Chicago's west side. In some ways I could relate to this teacher: White, female, and middle-class; when I began teaching I had limited experience working with students of color, in poverty, or with disabilities; minimal training in educational practices; often frustrated and looking for someone to blame, looking for answers, trying to understand. But in other ways, I struggled to understand her perspective: Her kids *can't* do grade level math? What does that mean?

In that moment, although I still had a ton to learn (and I still do), one thing I knew for sure: her kids absolutely *could*. It was her belief that they could not that was holding them back. I don't remember the exact course of our subsequent conversation except that I'm sure I bumbled around trying to "facilitate" a change in her beliefs about her students. I do remember that the teacher gave a lot of "right" answers, and I initially left feeling hopeful that we would see a change in her mindset, language, and behaviors. How naive I was in retrospect!

Untold Narratives, pages 121–125
Copyright © 2018 by Information Age Publishing
All rights of reproduction in any form reserved.

This same young woman would continue to make comments that blamed or sold her students short. I would continue to try and change her mindset. How could she not see the damage her own beliefs and practices caused her students, her relationships with families and her own teaching? She eventually quit. Unfortunately, as several of the stories in this edition have shown, she is not alone in her failure to believe in students' potential simply because they are students of color or students with disabilities (Blanchett, 2010). Both race and disability are largely social constructs. Teachers who believe, like this teacher, that there is something inherently "wrong" or "lacking" about a student who can be described as one or both of those constructs (Connor, Ferri, & Annamma, 2016) are perpetuating years of marginalization and ostracization that further perpetuate low academic achievement for African American students with disabilities (Fashola, 2005; Ferri & Connor, 2005; Polite & Davis, 1999).

Which is one of the many reasons why this book and the stories within it are so critical: to educate, challenge, enlighten, and potentially change teachers' beliefs, understanding and, hopefully, their actions towards and interactions with students and families. Perhaps hearing the experiences of being a student of color and of being identified as having a disability, from students, in their own words, can humanize our students a bit more, provide insight and empathy, and encouraged us to be more critical in examining our role in our students' educational experiences.

The truth is, comments like those made by the teacher above are racist, though that might have shocked the teacher who originally made them. It is likely that she, like many others, believes that we live in a post-racial, colorblind society where racism no longer exist, that racism is something overt, as from before the Civil Rights Movement. That racism is people burning crosses and yelling racial epithets. One only needs to look to Ferguson (2014) and Charleston (2015) and Charlottesville (2017) to know that racism in those overt forms still exist. But racism today is not limited to those overt actions! Racism also exists in historical and systemic legacies (see, *The New Jim Crow*, or *Segregation Now*) as well as, and more often via, insidious forms: hearing from teachers that "they can't," disproportionately being pulled over by police, redlining districts, being blacklisted for kneeling during the national anthem, limited representation across all major forms of media, and yes, overrepresentation in special education (Blanchett, Mumford, & Beachum, 2005).

According to Harry (2006), "Ethnic disproportionality in special education refers to the fact that students from certain historically excluded minority groups have been placed in special education programs at rates that are disproportionate to their presence in the student population as a whole" (p. 67). There are myriad reasons for this disproportionality, but all share at their core some level of discriminatory practices and/or history that need to be understood, challenged, and changed.

A majority of educators are White, middle-class, neurotypical females. As such, these educators have privileges that, if unacknowledged and unchallenged, can and will perpetuate the discriminatory practices Dr. Harry is describing. But even those educators who come from non-White, non-middle class, non-nuerotypical backgrounds still teach within historically biased systems. Reading and sharing *Untold Narratives* is a critical step toward assigning meaning to the socially constructed categories of difference marked by the intersection of ability, race, class, and gender (Blanchett, Klingner, & Harry, 2009).

The stories shared between these pages should serve to not only offer insight into these sociocultural patterns, but also serve as a call to action in order to directly address the societal problems stemming directly and indirectly from our country's history. Here are five additional actions educators, stakeholders, and those who care about education and equity can and should take upon finishing this volume:

AMPLIFY STUDENT (AND FAMILY) VOICES

Let me be clear—our job is NOT to "give" voice to students and families, as we are often told, but to amplify the voices they have. As these pages attest, our students have their own, insightful voices. We just have not been listening and we have not given platform to those voices. We must make space in our classrooms and communities for *all* voices to be heard.

EMPOWER FAMILIES

Education as a field has its own procedures, policies, and language. For example terms like *common core, formative,* and *response to intervention* all have specialized meaning to educators. This is before we even begin to layer on special education-specific terminology and acronyms like eligibility, LRE, and IEP. As educators, we must ensure that families understand us when we talk to them about their student(s) and their education. And we, in turn, need to listen to their ideas, knowledge, and questions. We must therefore speak in family-friendly language, translating our "eduspeak," and ensuring they are understanding as we go. We also need to create environments that are conducive to and which give opportunities for families to speak up and participate.

GET EDUCATED ABOUT DISCRIT

A close cousin of Critical Race Theory (CRT), DisCrit examines the intersection of race and disability, specifically the ways in which it reinforces racial hierarchies and eurocentric definitions of normalcy and ability. DisCrit seeks to critically evaluate the ways in which both race and ability are social constructs that serve to normalize and reinforce one another, that is, "racism validates and reinforces ableism, and ableism validates and reinforces racism" (Connor, Ferri, & Annamma, 2016). We must engage in critical reflection, with a specific focus on the intersection between race and ability. Critical reflection is a "stance that involves internalized habits of seeing the complexity of urban schools, seeing one's own assumptions and identity, and seeing the need for collaborative knowledge making practice that interrupts the dysfunctional and generates uncommon solutions" (Berghoff, Blackwell, & Wisehart, 2011, p. 27).

DEVELOP YOUR LIBERATORY CONSCIOUSNESS
(LOVE, 2000)

This means you engage in four related processes. First, you recognize or have *awareness* that there are systems and structures in place that continue to marginalize and take voice from people of color. For our students with disabilities, they are dually impacted. Second, you *analyze* the world, the systems, and the individuals (self-included) from that stance of awareness, especially focusing on your own role within those systems. Third, you *act* on this analysis. Sometimes you lead, sometimes you follow, and sometimes you offer support. And finally, you take *accountability*, meaning you take ownership for helping others on this same journey. As educators, this most often means our colleagues and other members of our personal lives.

LISTEN. SPEAK UP

Listen specifically to your students, their families, and to others whose voices are often silenced or listened to with skepticism. Speak up when you hear things that discount, marginalize, or otherwise demean your students or others like them, even when it is your own voice saying or thinking those things.

Only if we collectively work to *understand* and *act* can we begin to undo the effects of and correct the systems which have created and perpetuated inequities in access, opportunities, and achievement.

REFERENCES

Alexander, M. (2012). *The new Jim Crow: Mass incarceration in the age of colorblindness.* New York, NY: New Press.

Berghoff, B., Blackwell, S., & Wisehart, R. (2011). Using critical reflection to improve urban teacher preparation: A collaborative inquiry of three teacher educators. *Perspectives on Urban Education, 8*(2), 19–28.

Blanchett, J. W. (2010). Telling like it is: The role of race, class, & culture in the perpetuation of learning disability as a privileged category for the White middle class. *Disability Studies Quarterly, 30*(2). doi:http://dx.doi.org/10.18061/dsq.v30i2

Blanchett, W. J., Klingner, J. K., & Harry, B. (2009). The intersection of race, culture, language and disability: Implications for urban education. *Urban Education, 44*(4), 389–409.

Blanchett, W. J., Mumford, V., & Beachum, F. (2005). Urban school failure and disproportionality in a post-*Brown* era: Benign neglect of students of color's constitutional rights. *Remedial and Special Education, 26*(2), 70–81.

Connor, D. J., Ferri, B. A., & Annamma, S. A. (2016). *DisCrit: disability studies and critical race theory in education.* New York, NY: Teachers College Press.

Ferri, B. A., & Connor, D. (2005). Tools of exclusion: Race, disability and (re)segregated education. *Teachers College Record, 107*(3), 453–474.

Hannah-Jones, N. (2016, April 27). *Segregation now.* Retrieved from https://www.theatlantic.com/magazine/archive/2014/05/segregation-now/359813/

Harry, B. (2007). The disproportionate placement of ethnic minorities in special education. In L. Florian (Ed.). *The SAGE handbook of special education* (pp. 67–84). London, England: SAGE.

Howard, T. C. (2003). Culturally relevant pedagogy: Ingredients for critical teacher reflection. *Theory into Practice, 42*(3), 195–202.

Love, B. J. (2000). Developing a liberatory consciousness. In M. Adams et a. (Eds.) *Readings for diversity and social justice* (pp. 559–603). New York, NY: Routledge.

ABOUT THE EDITOR

Shawn Anthony Robinson, PhD is a dyslexia consultant whose research focuses on the intersection of race, giftedness and dyslexia. He brings a wealth of academic and personal experience, training and knowledge about the development of dyslexia. Robinson is recognized as an emerging scholar who addresses inequalities in the fields of Language and Literacy and Special Education, and has written numerous peer-reviewed publications.

Robinson graduated from the University of Wisconsin Oshkosh (UWO) with a Bachelor's of Science, a Master's in Education from DePaul University, and a PhD in Language and Literacy from Cardinal Stritch University. Robinson has received several distinguished honors throughout his early career such as: a recipient of New Trier High Schools 2017 Young Alumnus Award, a 2016 recipient of the Outstanding Young Alumni Award from UWO, served as a fellow for the 2015 8th Annual Asa G. Hilliard III and Barbara A. Sizemore Research Institute on African Americans and Education–American Educational Research Association, and the 2013 Achievement Gap Institute–Vanderbilt University Peabody College of Education & Human Development, and was also a recipient of All-State Insurance's 2005 Educator of the Year for the City of Chicago.

Robinson's work has been highlighted on NBC News in an article titled "This Man is Searching For a Link Between Illiteracy and Racial Bias." He currently lives in Wisconsin with his wife and sons. He loves spending time with his family, writing, and is a life member of Alpha Phi Alpha Fraternity, Inc.

ABOUT THE CONTRIBUTORS

Amar Abbott is a doctoral candidate at Pepperdine University's program in Learning Technologies. A native of Napa, California, Mr. Abbott has a Master's in Educational Technologies and a Bachelor's in Communication Studies with an emphasis Digital Media. For the past 13 years, Mr. Abbott has been instructing students with disabilities on the use of educational and assistive technologies, and he is currently an associate professor at Taft College located in Taft, California. Mr. Abbott is passionate about educational and employment access for people with disabilities and believes equal access to technology can positively affect their lives.

Dr. Aaliyah Baker is an Assistant Professor in the College of Education and Leadership at Cardinal Stritch University, Milwaukee, WI. She began her career in education as a classroom teacher with the Milwaukee Public Schools system. She earned her PhD in Curriculum and Instruction (University of Wisconsin–Madison). Her research interests include critical race theory, multicultural education, sociocultural theories of learning, and the role of race, class and gender in educational achievement and experiences in schools. She has conducted research within the scope of education, society, culture and learning in Morocco and South Africa as a Fulbright-Hays Group Projects Abroad grant recipient. Dr. Baker maintains a strong partnership with Jo's Learning Academy in Milwaukee, WI by developing and supporting curriculum, assessment, and instruction in primary grades.

Aunye' Boone hails from Southern Maryland and received her BA in English from Virginia Tech with a minor in philosophy. During her time at

Virginia Tech, she ran track on a full athletic scholarship, was VT Rookie of the Year, and nominated for VT Woman of the Year. Aunye' worked for Calvert County Public Schools as an Honors English Teacher and track coach, impacting the lives of the students with her compassion and ability to adjust and modify the Common Core curriculum to suit the needs of every learner. In the summer of 2011, Aunye' traveled to Vietnam with the program Coach for College to teach/coach underprivileged students, and gave them access to educational resources that they never had before. Having a passion for both the education and the arts, Aunye' has television, commercial, and stage credits. Taking part in the DC Women's Theatre Festival, Aunye' had the lead role in the Compass Rose Theatre production of *If I Hold My Tongue,* which was also performed as a staged reading at the Kennedy Center in the fall of 2015. In the fall of 2015, Aunye' was diagnosed with otosclerosis, a hereditary disease that causes gradual deafness. After receiving part 1 of her stapedectomy, she has regained partial hearing and became an advocate for the Hearing Loss Association of America.

Danyelle Cerillo was born and raised in Southern California. Her hobbies include singing, writing, and public speaking. She graduated from the University of Arizona in May 2013, with a major in Linguistics and a minor in Spanish. For the past 4 years, she has assisted blind children, youth and adults with Braille and independent living skills. These services have been provided at various organizations for the blind in Southern California. Her passion in life is to encourage others, and she believes that a person can do whatever they set their mind to, as well as live their lives to the fullest. As a young woman who has a disability, her motto for each day is live life to the fullest. Her future goal is to be a Spanish interpreter for crusades that share the gospel.

Oluwakemi (Kemi) Elufiede, MEd, educator, author, editor, poet, and entrepreneur, has over 10 years of professional experience in public, higher, community (education), non-profit sector, and social services. She is the Founder and President of Carnegie Writers, Inc. and K&E Educational Consulting Services, where she helps in writing, editing, non-profit management, life-coaching and publishing. Prior to entrepreneurship, Elufiede assumed many roles as a tutor, teacher, mentor, instructor, evaluations manager, case manager, and residence director. In these various roles, she implemented and facilitated programs for the improvement of literacy and writing skills; behavioral health and developmental disabilities; career and workforce development, and personal growth and development. She has presented at over 20 professional conferences/workshops and facilitated over 30 programs. She is currently a faculty member at Daymar College in Nashville, TN. She holds a degree in P–12 Special Education from Abraham

Baldwin Agricultural College, BLS in Psychology and MEd in Adult Education and Community Leadership from Armstrong Atlantic State University.

Rev. Russell Ewell serves as co-chair of The United Methodist Association of Ministers with Disabilities and Associate Pastor of The Village Church of St. Louis (UMC). His introduction to advocacy began with his enrollment into Kindergarten. Ophthalmologists and educators forewarned, "Blind students could not succeed in integrated classrooms." So "don't dream of one day seeing your son graduate from high school." Confounding conventional wisdom, he graduated from high school, earned a BS in Sociology, and is the first blind student to graduate from Eden Theological Seminary in its 168-year history. He's also the first blind person to be ordained in the Missouri Conference of the United Methodist Church. He gives talks across the country on Disability Advocacy and Awareness, The Disability Rights Movement, The Intersections of Religion and Disability, and The Intersectionality of Disability Theology and Black Theology. He works to empower the disenfranchised and assist all people to realize their potential, purpose and worth.

Jody Fields has a doctorate degree in Public Administration from Jackson State University in Jackson, Mississippi. She is the Director of the Center for Applied Studies in Education and the IDEA Data and Research Office. The IDEA Data and Research Office is a grant from the Arkansas Department of Education's Special Education Unit to provide quality data management, analysis, technical assistance, and research for the enhancement of the Arkansas Department of Education's general supervision of local education agencies' special education programs by ensuring accurate, valid, and timely data to meet all state and federal reporting. Dr. Fields also serves as the special education data manager for the past 14 years.

David Kennedy is currently an Adjunct Lecturer and a MPhil/PhD student in the School of Education at the University of the West Indies, Mona Campus. He was a double certified Special Educator in the states of Florida and Colorado, where he taught for six years. He holds both an MA in Curriculum and Instruction from the University of Denver, and a BSc in Public Relations and History from the University of Florida. His research interests include, but are not limited to: Hip Hop and the arts in urban education and reggae music and poetry as a vehicle for social change in the Caribbean and across the world.

Kristie Roberts-Lewis is an Adjunct Professor and University Research Reviewer with Walden University where she has served for the past 13 years. During her tenure with Walden, Dr. Roberts-Lewis has been recognized as a Bernard L. Turner Award Recipient (2017), the highest faculty award bestowed to a member of the dissertation committee of the student who was awarded the "Best Dissertation of the Year Award." Concomitantly, in this capacity Dr. Roberts-Lewis teaches doctoral and masters courses in Public Policy and Administration, serves as dissertation chairperson to dozens of PhD candidates and serves as a University Research Reviewer to ensure that Walden's standards of excellence are realized in all student dissertations. Additionally, Dr. Roberts-Lewis is the CEO/Founder of Women of Destiny and Distinction an organization designed to help empower, equip, and engage women and girls on the road to destiny and purpose.

Ronnie Sidney, II, LCSW, attended Essex County Public Schools, spending seven of twelve years in special education. Ronnie is a graduate of Old Dominion University (2006) and Virginia Commonwealth University (2014). In 2015, Ronnie published *Nelson Beats the Odds*, a semiautobiographical graphic novel about his experience in special education. Ronnie followed up with three more graphic novels, *Tameka's New Dress, Nelson Beats the Odds: Compendium One*, and *Rest in Peace RaShawn*. In 2015, Sidney developed the "Nelson Beats the Odds Comic Creator" app to help young people celebrate their strengths and feel good about themselves. Ronnie has appeared on MichaeLA, NPR, Fox and Friends Weekend, and NBC 12 News.

Saran Stewart is a Lecturer of Comparative Higher Education in the School of Education at the University of the West Indies, Mona Campus. She is also the coordinator for the MA in Higher Educational Management programme and chief editor of the *Journal of Education and Development in the Caribbean*. Much of her research uses quantitative, qualitative, and mixed methods to critically examine issues of comparative education, postcolonial theories, critical—inclusive pedagogy and access/equity issues in higher education. Dr. Stewart is devoted to the examination and exploration of topics related to access and equity in education and teaching and learning in developing country contexts. With more than eighteen refereed scholarly articles, book chapters and an edited book, her work has been published in the *Journal of Diversity in Higher Education, Journal of Student Affairs, Postcolonial Directions in Education Journal*, and the *Applied Anthropologist Journal*, to name a few. Dr. Stewart most recently received the University of the West Indies, Principals Award for Most Outstanding Researcher and Best Publication (Article Category). She holds a BA with honors in English and International Studies, a MBA in Marketing, an MA in International Administration and a PhD in Higher Education.

Nina F. Weisling was a special and general educator in Philadelphia and Chicago. She later worked as an induction coach and co-manager of the induction team while she earned her doctorate in Special Education from the University of Illinois at Chicago. She currently works as an assistant professor of special education in the Teacher Education Division at Cardinal Stritch University in Milwaukee, WI. Her research interests include training and support of urban educators, particularly special and general educators who work with students with disabilities.

CPSIA information can be obtained
at www.ICGtesting.com
Printed in the USA
LVOW13s1149280218
568111LV00006B/35/P